Sept. 30, 1994 — Frankfort

The Struggle to Believe

Rethinking Faith
for the Twenty-first Century

The Struggle to Believe

Rethinking Faith for the Twenty-first Century

William L. Turner

Smyth & Helwys Publishing, Inc.
Macon, Georgia

ISBN 1-880837-28-5

The Struggle to Believe

William L. Turner

Copyright © 1993
Smyth & Helwys Publishing, Inc.
Macon, Georgia

All rights reserved.

Printed in the United States of America.

The paper used in this publication meets the minimum
requirements of American Standard for Information
Sciences—Permanence of paper for Printed Library Materials,
ANSI Z39.48–1984.

Library of Congress Cataloging-in-Publication Data

Turner, William L., 1938–
The struggle to believe / William L. Turner.
x+134pp.   6x9" (15x23 cm.)
Includes bibliographical references.
ISBN 1-880837-28-5 (alk. paper)
1. Apologetics—20th century. I. Title.
BT1102.T875   1993
239—dc20   93-713
                                         CIP

Contents

Preface vii

Introduction 1

1. Who Am I? 7

2. Is There a God? 15

3. Where Is God When People Hurt? 27

4. What Is the Meaning of Life? 41

5. How Does Faith Work? 53

6. But Aren't Saviors for Weaklings? 65

7. Haven't We Outgrown Sin? 77

8. So Who Needs the Church? 91

9. Is Prayer for Real? 103

10. What Happens When We Die? 117

Epilogue 131

Notes 133

Preface

What is written here is, essentially, testimony. For me, the search for meaningful faith starts and continues in personal relationship with God. It is not, however, a journey of isolation. The congregations of Central Baptist Church in Lexington, Kentucky, and South Main Baptist Church in Houston, Texas, have been my most recent companions on the way. Much of *The Struggle to Believe* they have shared in sermon and pastoral experience.

Our daughters, Lisa, Laurie, and Andrea, have been a constant source of encouragement as I have written these pages. "How's it going?" became both challenge and affirmation as they urged me to complete the project. Kelli, my wife of thirty-four years, has been my best critic and my strongest supporter.

My thanks to Scott Nash of Smyth & Helwys for his confidence and friendship. Thanks also to Martha Schneider, pastoral secretary and staff colleague at South Main Baptist Church, for her diligent and efficient work in typing and re-typing the manuscript. And special thanks to Laurie Turner, artist and daughter, whose thoughtful sketches are so descriptive of the struggle . . . and the rich possibilities . . . of Christian faith.

William L. Turner
Houston, Texas
Spring 1993

TO KELLI
Wife, lover, friend, and co-struggler in Christ

Introduction

"You're writing a book?" she asked.

She was the housekeeper for some friends in whose mountain home my wife and I were enjoying a fall vacation. "Uh huh," I responded. "About what?" she wanted to know. "Well, it deals with some of the hard and ongoing questions of life," was my response.

Silence, as she puttered in the kitchen next door to my writing table.

Then, "They really *are* hard. Why is there so much trouble? And, how can God be good when so many people are hurting?"

She *knew*! We'd met only a few hours earlier, and our conversations had been mostly small talk. She had seen neither my notes nor a table of contents, yet she knew the direction I intended for my writing.

A wild guess?

Maybe, but I think not. Matthew Arnold told us that "the same heart beats in every human breast." The great, tough questions not only bind us together in a struggle for answers, but they put the whole issue of faith at risk. Because, whether you acknowledge it or not, such musings are intensely spiritual in nature. They beg entry to our wills and hearts, as well as our minds. They force us to grapple all our lives through with those ever-hovering concerns of purpose . . . direction . . . and destiny. Hence, Paul Tillich's sound judgment that life's most "religious questions" are invariably raised—even by "irreligious" people:

> What is the meaning of life?
> Where do we come from; where do we go?
> What shall we do?
> What should we become in the short stretch
>   between birth and death?

The search for knowing and believing is not new. Back in the eighteenth century, Immanuel Kant said that there are but three questions: What can I know? What ought I to do? What can I hope? And Sigmund Freud, an atheist himself, admitted that the oldest, deepest, most urgent desires of humanity arise in religion.

But is faith possible?

For many people, obviously, it is. It's been around for centuries and in a wide variety of expressions. But just now, as we move toward the twenty-first century, the question looms larger, "How believable is belief?"

In America, I don't hear any funeral dirges for generic faith-in-God, but I do hear voices of protest, apathy, and desertion raised against "Christian orthodoxy." It seems to me that, fairly often, this attack or retreat gets framed as a question. An *emotional* crisis leaves scars, and the questions follow: "Where is God when people hurt?" "How does faith work, if at all?" "Is prayer for real?" "What happens when we die?" Or an *intellectual* impasse demands fresh answers to old questions: "Is there a God?" "What is the meaning of life?" "Haven't we outgrown sin?" "Who needs the church?"

Such traditional religious language still holds meaning for many people. But I encounter a growing number who hunger for a fresh experience with God and for a fresh *understanding* of that experience. For these individuals, orthodox frames of reference may be a childhood memory, but they mean little during the mature years without a faith that is both intellectually defensible and spiritually satisfying.

So my purpose in this volume is to listen to some of the enduring questions, suggest some answers, and join the reader in his/her struggle to believe. Three disclaimers at the outset, if you please. First, I make no assumptions about absolute knowledge—except that I do not possess it. I have found—or been found by—satisfying answers to these enduring questions. Yet because God is Mystery and I am finite, there is forever more to learn. Faith is not only an affirmation of belief; it is journey into knowing.

Also, I do not stand or speak or write in isolation. I belong to a family of particular religious tradition—Christian, biblical, historical, and reformed. The plausible answers that shape my life have come to me largely from that tradition. Therefore, I am child of what I've been handed . . . what I've discarded . . . and what I've finally claimed for myself.

Third, as I hope you've already guessed, my answers are more confessional than argumentative. I dare to hope that my words may strike a responsive chord in you, so that—human as they are—they may yet become a word from God to your life.

Some years back, I wrote to a young man in our city, introducing myself as his parents' friend and inviting him to attend our church. His response, measured and gracious, contained these words:

> Although I appreciate your invitation, I must tell you that I can no longer be comfortable in the Baptist church. I find that too many mysteries are defined too rigidly for me to maintain my internal consistency.

That's a legitimate challenge to every pulpit—Baptist or otherwise. It's also a challenge to such pages as now lie before you. Certainly some of the worst abuses of religion have sprung from the idolizing of "truth," narrowly perceived. Thus, I do not intend to *overdefine* God or to *overstate* my faith to the exclusion of everybody else's.

I *do*, however, mean to say "Here I stand," as clearly as I possibly can. In response to a friendly critic who commented, "It's been said better before," Madeleine L'Engle said, "Of course, It's all been said better before. If I thought I had to say it better than anybody else, I'd never start. Better or worse is immaterial. The thing is that it has to be said; by me. . . ."[1] Backgrounded against the possibilities of God, I struggle with the possibilities of my human situation. And I aim to tell you where my search has led . . . is leading.

Who knows? At book's end, maybe you and I can stand together. Read on . . . and see!

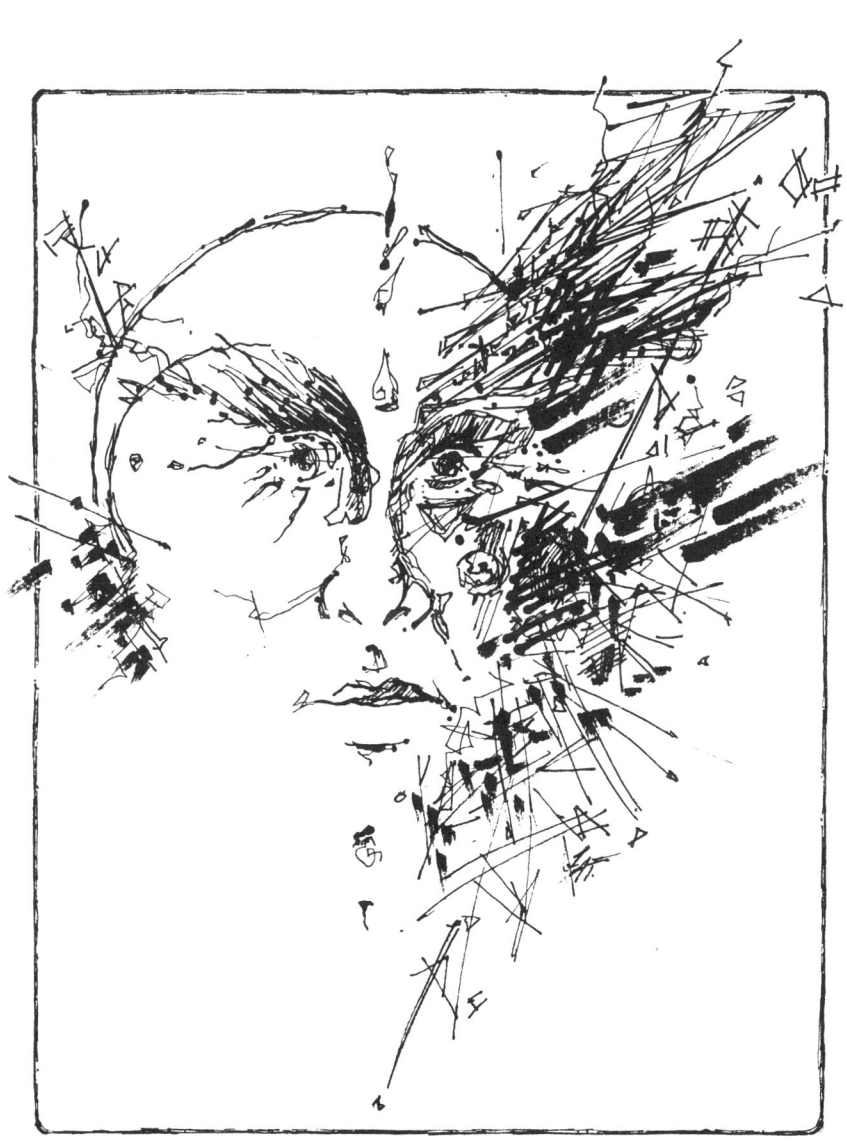

Chapter One

"Who Am I?"

Psalm 8

During her teenage years, our youngest daughter often cornered her mother and me with the request, "Tell me something funny I did as a child. What do you remember that I don't?"

Over the years I've decided that such curiosity is more than a matter of roots and memories; it's a search for identity. To be sure, none of us need be trapped in the past, but as family stories get told and retold, our images of self-identity get sharpened and refined.

"Who am I?" is the uniquely human question. Only our kind of creature turns philosophical over personal identity. In a Peanuts comic strip, Snoopy the dog reflects on his "dogginess":

> I wonder why some of us were born dogs while others were born people. . . . Is it pure chance or what is it? . . . Somehow, the whole thing doesn't seem very fair. . . . Why should *I* have been the lucky one?[1]

Contemplative dogs and cats exist in cartoons—and we love it— but in the real world the ponderings of selfhood belong to the human animal. Such pondering lies at the heart of the old Hebrew hymn that is the eighth psalm. On a long-ago star-filled night, someone was feeling awe and wonder:

> When I look at thy heavens, the work of thy fingers,
>   the moon and the stars which thou hast established;
> what is man that thou art mindful of him,
>   and the son of man that thou dost care for him? (vs. 3-4)

Man—generic, collective, inclusive of both sexes—what are we to make of man? We are so finite against the infinity of space . . . such tiny, mortal drops in so vast a cosmic bucket. "Where does humankind fit into the scheme of all that is?" this biblical writer wants to know. And, modern as we 1990s people are, we continue to struggle with the question.

Of course, there are several ways to answer. We may define ourselves *sexually*; we are male and we are female. We may be identified *vocationally*—our *who*-ness being defined by the *how*-ness of earning a living. There is, obviously, a *biological* answer. Man is a physical conglomeration of three and a half million parts . . . with a heart that beats more than 40,000 times a day . . . and a digestive system that allows a teenager to consume at least a million calories a year!

Also, there's an *intellectual* answer to our question. Industrialist Benjamin Fairless died before today's computer craze took hold, but he saw from afar the coming worship of high-tech capability. He once ventured that if the apple that fell on Isaac Newton's head had fallen on a computer, the machine might've blown a tube . . . but it wouldn't have come up with the law of gravity! Without doubt, we'll continue to render to the (now tube-less) computer what is the computer's . . . but the human mind is a rare and precious gift. It affords all the multidimensional possibilities of curiosity, reason, thought, language, and choice that are unique to our kind.

In combining biology and intelligence, there's yet another facet to human identity; namely, our *creativity*. In the fall of 1957, the city of Chicago invited Carl Sandburg to a celebration of the city's progress. A United Press International dispatch contained his commentary:

> When one tall skyscraper is torn down
> To make room for a taller one to go up
> Who takes down and puts up those skyscrapers?
> Man—the little two-legged joker—MAN.[2]

The great cities, the beautiful symphonies, the priceless paintings, the enduring cultures . . . all are the fruits of our creaturely creativity.

In addition to all these ways of viewing our humanity, there is at least one other facet. In any composite of humankind, it should not be omitted. Hear again our ancient psalmist:

> Yet thou hast made him little less than God,
>   and dost crown him with glory and honor.
> Thou hast given him dominion over the works of thy hands;
>   thou hast put all things under his feet,
>   all sheep and oxen,
>   and also the beasts of the field,
>   the birds of the air, and the fish of the sea,
>   whatever passes along the paths of the sea. (vs. 5-8)

And the song is bracketed, start and finish, with this refrain:

> O Lord, our Lord,
> how majestic is thy name in all the earth. (vs. 1, 9)

So . . . whatever else we may be, there is this linkage to God. That's a faith assumption, all right, but I think our Hebrew hymnist is right in sync with reality. Measure humankind by all the other yardsticks, but if you leave out our *spiritual* possibilities, you've missed a critical part of the story. Of all our human qualities, none is more intriguing than that we are God's "next of kin" in the cosmos. Nothing about us is more breathtaking than that we hold the potential for conscious partnership with the Eternal One! In the Genesis creation story, the Hebrew word for "man" is *adham*, while the word for "ground" is *adhamah* (cf. Gen 2:7). The word play is obvious. I am earthy and physical (made from "the dust of the ground"), but I am also that being/soul from the hand and image of God ("the great amphibian" was Sir Thomas Browne's descriptive phrase).

In his famous Sistine Chapel painting, Michelangelo captures the essence of human identity. Adam reclines, his hand limp, while the muscular, dynamic figure of God moves toward him. Within seconds the tense finger of God will touch the listless finger of man, and you can easily anticipate the result. Something powerful . . . life-giving . . . electric is going to happen! The point is clear: full humanity requires the touch of God, and without it we are incomplete.

The biblical answer to "Who am I?" then, is that I am the unique creature capable of being *responsive* to the Creator and *responsible* in my use of "the works of" his creation (cf. Ps 8:6; Gen 1:27–30). Hence, ecology and "earth ethics" were not born in the twentieth century; they're as old as life itself. We men and women *are* sexual, biological, intellectual, and creative creatures.

Still, if we are no more than gifted, two-legged accidents who are headed for extinction, "identity" and "purpose" are pretty hollow words. In "Rugby Chapel," Matthew Arnold voices a lament over such emptiness of existence:

> What is the course of the life
> Of mortal men on the earth?
> Most men eddy about
> Here and there—eat and drink,
> Chatter and love and hate,
> Gather and squander, are raised
> Aloft, are hurled in the dust,
> Striving blindly, achieving
> Nothing; and then they die—
> Perish—and no one asks
> Who or what they have been,
> More than he asks what waves,
> In the moonlit solitudes mild
> Of the midmost Ocean, have swelled,
> Foamed for a moment, and gone.

If our timebound lives can be rooted in some Reality deeper than the merely material, however, then full human identity becomes an exciting possibility.

Now, unlike all other created beings, I am free to accept or reject a relationship with the Creator. Thus, the touch of the Eternal upon my life can be pushed aside if I so choose. That, too, is part of the Bible's definition of our humanity. Created "in the image of God," we are given a sovereignty similar to our Maker's. We may say "no" to any conscious partnership and proceed to live life on our own. "Sin" is the biblical word for that choice. "Gone astray" and "fallen short of the glory of God" are the familiar phrases (cf. Isa 53:6; Rom 3;23). What does it mean? That God is either ignored or pushed aside. That my life gets centered in and defined by myself, period. That, with God out of the partnership picture, all prerogatives become mine.

What emerges in daily living from such a choice turns out to be pretty selfish and shallow, ugly and harsh, apathetic and empty. We shut God out of our lives, then wonder why human existence seems hollow. Kierkegaard called sin "the despairing refusal to be oneself." Adrift from our spiritual mooring, there's no way to experience our truest humanness.

In time we seek to fill the void with other things. We work out and diet. We consult the stars. We fill up houses and garages and second homes with things. We work incessantly or play feverishly. And all the while there is a gnawing and knowing that refuses to go away. Deep down, like Captain Ahab, what we need is "something in this slippery world that can hold." We hunger and thirst for a *centering* that—like a magnet pulling metal filings—will draw the scattered pieces of our lives into some kind of wholeness.

And, it is God who gives us exactly what we need.

If our sin means separation from God and full humanness, *God's love* means reconciliation and fresh possibility. To our waywardness, God speaks forgiveness . . . and he speaks it best in a "Word made flesh" (cf. John 1:14). The amazing message of the Bible is that the Eternal One reaches to touch us at last in One-like-us named Jesus of Nazareth . . . that is, in the language of a singular human life. In Jesus, not only do I see my selfhood as it was meant to be, but I see God's love as the healing agent for my fragmented and frustrated life. Recalling his life, death, and resurrection, 1 Corinthians 15 appropriately refers to Christ as "the last Adam." This means that nothing less than a new humanity opens to me through faith in Jesus Christ. God's forgiving love—shown most clearly in Christ—would reaffirm me as partner and friend . . . would center my living and working . . . and would let fall the barriers between me and the others whom God has made.

One Sunday morning, while I was preaching on how God creates and loves us, a small child in the pew leaned up to her father and said, "He's right, Dad. If you go to the trouble to make something with your own hands, you really *do* care about it."

To our "Who am I?" question, that little girl's comment suggests a great answer. You are God's creation. You have eternal worth and infinite possibility. Best of all, the One whose hands shaped your beginning would now touch you in love and in restoration.

Our faith-journey can start with this kind of answer. But that raises the larger issue of God. Is God believable?

Chapter Two

"Is There a God?"

Exodus 3:1–15

She was a bright adolescent. I was the visiting preacher for the special services in her southern Indiana church. Her pastor and I sat in the living room of her home, talking with her about the possibility of faith in Jesus Christ. Early in that conversation, and with refreshing honesty, she said, "Tell me, how can I know that God really exists?" I recall now that we discussed the question for a good while that Saturday afternoon. I do not recall that she chose to become a Christian believer during that revival week. Her question, however, is one of the enduring ones.

"Is there a God?"

It seems to grow out of our anthropology as much as our theology. Most everywhere you find the human creature, you find also a yearning directed toward something/someone beyond. The analysis of human societies, complex or simple, consistently reveals the need to somehow connect with a higher being or beings. We are, as the Greek term suggests, *anthropoi*—the upward-looking ones.

Human reason responds to our question with answers pro and con. Years ago, Julian Huxley prophesied the time when it would be as impossible for an intelligent person to believe in God as to believe in a flat earth. In his brilliant mind, humanity required no power/presence beyond our own wisdom and intelligence. Bertrand Russell declared that what science cannot tell us we cannot know, suggesting the all sufficiency of our human powers . . . and eliminating the necessity of deity.

Others, however, have launched various rational "arguments" *for* the existence of God. Archbishop Anselm (11th century, A.D.) ventured that our minds demand something higher and greater than themselves, and God is that being than which no greater or higher can be conceived. Thus, he reasoned, God is. Over the centuries, other rationales have been given. We thirst; water exists. We hunger; there is food. We have sexual appetites; there is the opposite sex. We have spiritual needs; there is God. One favorite argument for God's existence reasons back from the cosmos to the Creator. An orderly universe presupposes an Orderer . . . hence, God is proven.

I doubt that such "arguments" are very convincing to objective observers. I confess that there's a lot in the cosmos that seems random and irrational to me (especially the precipitous wiles of Mother Nature—earthquakes, hurricanes, tornadoes, and floods, to name a few). Some things, however, give striking evidence of a wise creativity behind them—from the intricate design of a flower, to the predictable details of a human cell, to the measurable wonders of a vast ocean. Such reasoning helps me some, but maybe because I'm largely untutored in the sophisticated rubrics of modern science—or because I'm predisposed to theistic belief.

Whether or not rational discussion on the existence of God has value or not, the whole issue comes down to this: "I believe in God" is a *faith* assumption/affirmation. I know of no objectively verifiable proof for God's existence that would satisfy all inquirers. With the Genesis writer, I *believe* that "in the beginning God created the heavens and the earth," but there were no human eyewitnesses present at the birth of universe.

Twentieth-century investigation has, however, put us in the position to begin speaking scientifically of the *creation* of the cosmos. For instance, the "big bang" theory, along with its various modifications, argues for the rapid outward expansion of the universe. Is the radiation that is detectable in all parts of the heavens left over from a cataclysmic blast some twenty billion years ago? Such a blast would have hurled debris across the vast reaches of space. The theory is that some of those fragments became the Milky Way with its hundred billion stars. One of those stars is our sun, with its tiny scattering of planets revolving around it. This viewpoint, at least, suggests that our world and what we know of our universe could be the aftermath of a giant fireball eruption that occurred at a specific time far back in prehistory. Then, after millions of cooling-down years, unique two-legged creatures began to inhabit this sphere of cosmic shrapnel . . . and human life took shape.

Now, no scientist can prove conclusively that this is the way it happened. Nor can any scientist or theologian prove conclusively that it was God whose hand shaped such a creative process. It is now arguable, however, that the cosmos did have a creation point—that *something* generated the radioactive mass that would spark any explosion—and that somehow the process of creation-time was moved forward dramatically to allow for the survival of human life. Because, out of the gaseous and icy womb of prehistoric reality, there emerged a race able to tolerate and thrive in this planet's atmosphere. It's obvious that these creatures used reason as well as instinct, and thus they began to claim some control over their own destiny.

One of my favorite authors is Loren Eiseley, anthropologist and poet. His observation is that in order for human life to have occurred at all, some remarkable things had to happen "way back when." The brain had to triple in size rapidly, following birth. So a dramatic increase in the blood supply to the brain was necessary. Then childhood had to lengthen so that the brain could learn what others had learned before it. So the growth rate had to change drastically. Finally, family bonding had to happen so that this fragile new creature could be spared and prepared for adulthood. What was also required, wrote Eiseley, was that these changes take place either simultaneously or at a closely interwoven pace. Given the necessity of such radical biological/sociological changes, plus a sometimes-hostile natural environment, it's truly amazing that our kind even survived![1]

All of this happened, it seems to me, either by sheer accident or by patient design. So you have to make a faith assumption. The chain of causality rattles back to God, or it rattles back to cosmic luck. I've decided that it was God who lighted whatever ancient fuse ignited the cosmos . . . and that God's hands shaped the emerging, evolutionary process that resulted in human life as we now know it.

You can argue otherwise, and many people do. You can insist that there is no final, objective proof for my position, and you are correct. But human life on this planet as the *accidental* gathering of atoms and climate and gravity and balance is more than I can rationally swallow!

Still, I think I understand the atheism or agnosticism of some of my friends. Their arguments against the existence of deity seem formidable. "God is irrelevant," some would say. Maybe people needed God when they couldn't get answers to questions from other sources, but things are different now. A confident scientism and a comfortable humanism handle most of our needs nicely. Perhaps God was crucial for a more primitive, superstitious time, but we are now mature enough to cast off the God-domination of our past.

"God is out of date," say others. Usually this means that God remains locked up in those childhood or adolescent images from yesteryear. God is recalled as a "big Parent" who dictates rules, squelches thought, and scrutinizes behavior—especially whatever is fun! Or, God is viewed as a "control tower" who pushes the cosmic buttons, but is wholly impersonal. I like Reuel Howe's term, "god scraps." I'm convinced that the typical American's understanding of God is just such a Raggedy Ann collection of such scraps. We gather them from personal history, from culture, from folk ways, from superstitions and traditions, and from other people's misconceptions. Still, such a collage passes for definition with many persons . . . and God seems out of date.

"God is incompetent," yet others have decided. It's hard to square a caring God with a suffering planet (more about that in Chapter Three). In our more lucid, objective moments, we admit that most of our pain is tied up with our humanity—its freedom, vulnerability, and judgment. Yet we often feel the need to blame someone for the evil that befalls us, and God is available. Oscar Wilde once said that there was enough misery in any street in London to disprove God, and pessimistic English poet James Thomson voiced a bitterness known to many in "The City of Dreadful Night":

> Who is most wretched in this dolorous place?
>   I think myself; yet I would rather be
> My miserable self than he, than He
>   Who formed such creatures to his own disgrace.

> . . . I vow
>
>> That not for all Thy power furled and unfurled,
>>> For all the temples to Thy glory built,
>> would I assume the ignominious guilt
>>> Of having made such men in such a world.

As a pastoral counsellor, I sometimes hear faith rejected in such an angry and strident manner. More often I hear it rejected in sadness—a sort of throw-up-your-hands-in-despair kind of heaviness.

So, our emotional and intellectual struggles lead some of us to paint God out of the picture altogether. But where does that leave us?

Obviously, it leaves us *alone* in the cosmos. It means that creation is mindless and void of direction. It means that we are on earth purely by chance. And it follows that fate, luck, or coincidence are (to recall the words of an Albert Camus character) "our only reasonable divinities."

The absence of God also leaves us *limited*. Despite the life-improving power of today's technology, man as the master of his/her fate doesn't work very well. We haven't proven terribly successful at building a world of justice and goodness and peace. In many cases, our ignorance . . . our greed . . . our misguided zeal have turned the promises of Eden into disaster. Ruling God out of life leaves us shut up in a world where we are the only resources for living . . . and that's awfully limited.

The debate goes on. The arguments proliferate. In the final analysis we are left with the faith that God is or God is not. Is there a God? To answer "No" as much as "Yes" is, finally, a personal *credo*.

My *credo* is "Yes," and it's based on a couple of convictions. The ancient biblical story of Moses at the burning bush brings both of them into focus. First, *God is mystery*. Out of that desert encounter comes something awesome: "Go to Egypt. Tell Pharaoh to turn the Hebrew slaves loose. Bring them here to this mountain, Moses. You be their leader."

Now, if Moses is going to take such an assignment, he'd better have somebody else's name alongside his on the project. "Who are you?" he asks at the burning bush. "I Am Who I Am" is the response. God's name is a mysterious verb! In fact, that's how the understanding of God developed among the Hebrews. God revealed himself as one who *acted* in their history. "I Am Who I Am" can also be translated "I Cause to Be," or "I Will Be Who I Will Be." Personally, I think that the Exodus writer intended to leave it vague, open to a broad range of possibilities. The mystery remains, even in the giving of God's name. It's as if God is telling Moses, "Some of the answers will come later. For now, trust me to be the God who cares for you and will stand beside you." I doubt that our Hebrew storyteller is being evasive; he's just telling how it actually is with us and God. Augustine said that it's no wonder we can't fully comprehend God. If we could, he wouldn't be God.

But there *are* bushes that burn with the presence of God . . . in our lives . . . scattered along the way. When they do, we see momentarily into the great mystery. As difficult and risky as it may be to generalize encounter with God, there are experiences common to us all that help to penetrate. There is the love of a spouse or friend . . . a telescope fixed on the heavens . . . the smell of the woods after a rain . . . an unexpected moment of joy . . . hot, honest tears over happenings that turn into blessings . . . the birth or adoption of your child . . . the deepening that follows after pain and disappointment. Sometimes life's bushes burn with partial recognition of the Mystery who is certainly beyond us, yet breaking into our awareness from time to time.

So, my second conviction is that God is knowable. "Say this to the people of Israel, 'I Am has sent me to you'" (Exod 3:14). There's a bushel of mystery and uncertainty in that, but God goes on to give an additional piece of information as well:

> Say this . . . "The Lord, the God of your fathers, the God of Abraham, the God of Isaac, and the God of Jacob, has sent me to you": this is my name forever, and thus I am to be remembered throughout all generations. (vs. 15)

Despite the mystery, something is known. "Moses, I'm the God who called Abraham to walk by faith, who preserved Isaac's life, who struggled to make Jacob more then a trickster."

The uncertainty about God is far from total because apparently he elects to be recognized and understood by what he does in the lives of persons who choose partnership with him. There's a word for this in theology—revelation—and it means God's eagerness to show us himself. You see, the use of logic and rational argument may become a stimulating intellectual quest for God. It may even take us far down the path toward a meaningful relationship with God, but it will always stop short. William Temple described this pilgrimage well when he said that our purely natural attempts to understand God would end in a hunger that they *alone* cannot satisfy. Ultimately, then, if there's to be a divine-human relationship, there has to be some movement from God's side. Instead of waiting for us to find him, God must come to us.

And, it is my conviction that God approaches us most precisely and personally in the life of Jesus Christ.

Choosing not to stand aloof, God instead stands in with us by living our kind of life in the humanity of Jesus. With the apostle Paul, I believe that we have been given "the knowledge of the glory of God in the face of Christ" (2 Cor 4:6). Jesus certainly doesn't exhaust the mystery of God (indeed, the very possibility of incarnation generates mystery and wonder aplenty!). But because God-in-Christ has come within the scope of our understanding, there is much we *can* know. Jesus' life, death, and resurrection tell us that God's very nature is to love, to forgive, to make us his partners in shaping this world. The model of Jesus calls us to think God's thoughts after him in healing diseases, feeding the hungry, making peace, and otherwise caring for the cosmos and its inhabitants.

As mortals we "know in part," but the Christian confidence is that whatever is yet to be known about God, he will never be *less* than what Jesus has revealed him to be. If God is the ongoing film, the historical Jesus is the frozen frame that lets us see what the show's about. If God is the living organism, Jesus is the biopsy in which we examine the divine tissue. The essence of God has been made clear in that singular lifetime out of Nazareth. Now we know that God invites the peoples of our planet, and any other planets, to his love and comradeship.

God is mystery. God is knowable. A paradox? Yes, but the resolution lies in the *inside* look. The sanctuary of South Main Baptist Church in Houston, Texas, has some of the most beautiful stained-glass windows in our city. But if you stand outside, they appear dark, unclear, and mysterious. Come inside, however, when the sunlight shines through . . . and each window is ablaze with beauty, individuality, and clarity.

About the mystery of God, Jesus says, "Come inside. I am the door. Enter through me and take a look around. Ask your questions. Think your thoughts. Stretch your awareness. Grow your faith." Starting with eyes of faith on Christ, the journey into God can be reassuring and comforting. It can be open-ended and exciting as well!

The struggle to believe, however, inevitably leads into "the valley of the shadow" of suffering and evil. If faith is to mean anything to us, it must meet us in that valley. It must also help us move beyond it. To the subject of God and our troubles we must now turn.

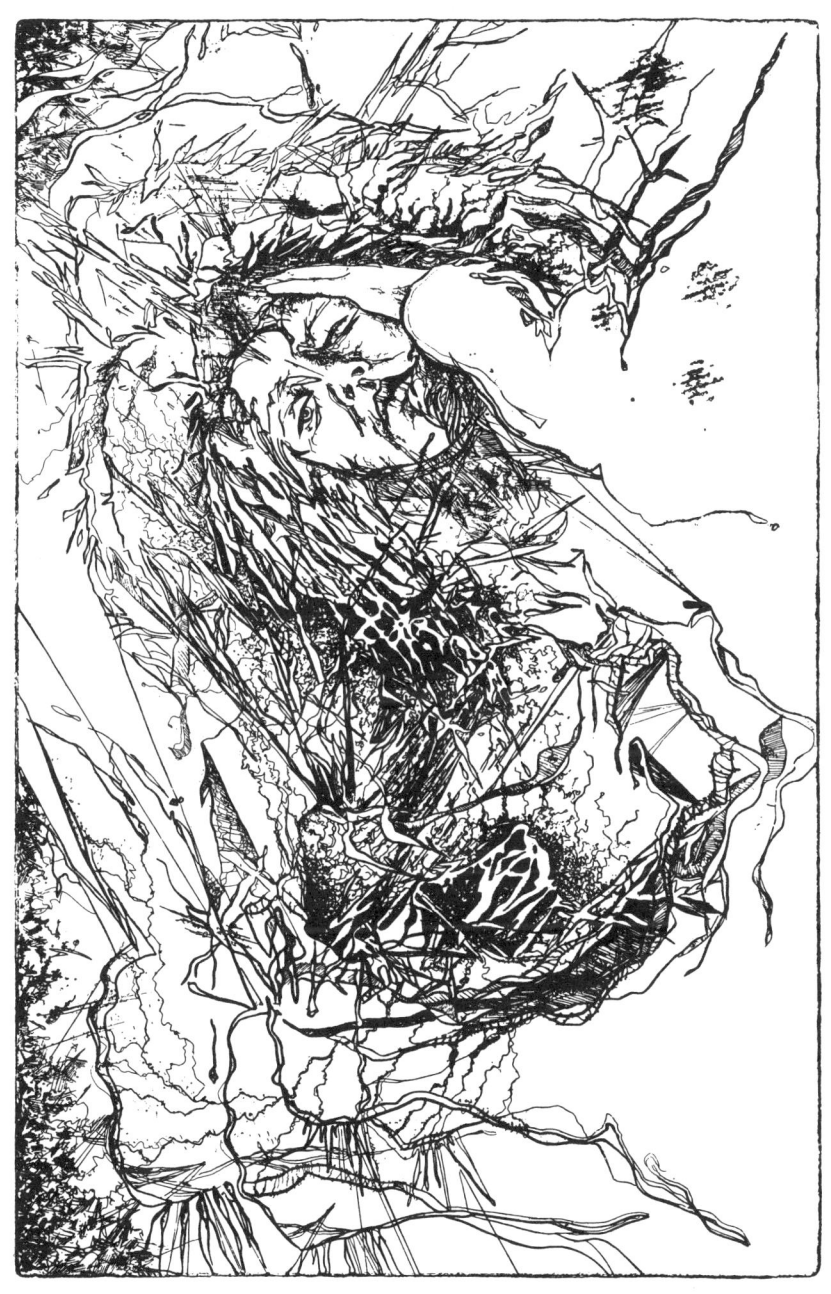

Chapter Three
"Where Is God When People Hurt?"
Romans 8:18-39

I recall a Simon and Garfunkel song that began:

> In my little town, I grew up believing
> God keeps his eye on us all.

And the refrain concluded:

> Nothing but the dead and dying
> Back in my little town.

The sense of it was that God is fond memory and nothing more. God has gone the way of other childhood fantasies, and we're now on our own. A spiritual homeland has been left, and, though there's a touch of wistfulness about that, we are finally a secular society. This is the age of "God Emeritus."

Is this really who we are?

The answer depends on who "we" are, I think. Blaise Paschal, the seventeenth-century scientist and philosopher, said you could divide all of us into three groups: those who know God and love him, those who don't know God but seek him, and those who neither know God nor seek him. Even in the 1990s that remains a pretty accurate assessment. If God has lost ground in this era, it's not a total loss. For most of us the yearning to know or love or seek remains strong.

But that yearning often runs aground on the harsh rocks of reality.

There has been an eclipse of the sun, one of those not-to-be missed events, and in *Peanuts* Lucy says to Linus, "What's this about not being able to look at the eclipse?" Linus replies, "It's very dangerous . . . you could suffer severe burns of the retina from infrared rays." Lucy says, "But what's the sense of having an eclipse if you can't look at it? Somebody in production sure slipped up this time!"[1]   That is often the trouble with reality . . . *and* with God.

A hurricane slams into an island country or an inland city, killing people and destroying property. An earthquake crushes out life between layers of highways and buildings. A young minister is shot dead in a downtown Houston church. A college coed is murdered. A space shuttle explodes, and the crew is lost. A nuclear meltdown spills poison radiation into the air. Ten thousand people starve to death in a single day. Six million Jews choke in the ovens of Europe. Nearly half of Cambodia's population is exterminated. We're stunned and stumped by cancer cells and AIDS viruses and tornadoes and birth defects, and the beat goes on: "Somebody in production sure slipped up."

"Somebody" is spelled G-O-D for a lot of people, and it's not because human hurt lacks logical, objective explanation. It's just that it's hard to say "We're in pain" and "God is love" in the same breath.

In the musical version of "Les Miserables," the chain-gang prisoners sang their opening chorus: "Sweet Jesus, hear my prayer." Then they sang: "Sweet Jesus *doesn't care*." Thus, one way of dealing with the problem is to discount faith totally and to expect zero help in crisis from God or anything that smacks of God. "Practical atheism" need not rule out deity altogether. God as Creative Power or Prime Mover of the cosmos may be logical enough. Even incarnation—God's entry into time-space history to declare his redemptive intention toward individuals—may seem believable. But the rest of life seems out of control at times. So if we do believe in God, it's pretty hard to say exactly how. George Sweazey wrote somewhere that if God is an "It," there really aren't too many atheists. Our problem is with God as a "You." Trying to square a just God—let alone One billed as personal and loving—with the tragedies of life is not easy. Some people who profess faith in God *have* squared it to their own liking. They have taken refuge in one of two very different positions: *naturalism* or *authoritarianism*.

The *naturalists* claim that though God created the universe, he is no longer connected with it—except through the indirect means of "natural law" (a term, by the way, which would have been meaningless to biblical characters like Abraham, Jacob, Peter, and Paul). God made what is, but chooses a sort of divine indifference to its ongoing life. He is an absentee landlord, and we are left alone with the workings of a purely materialistic/naturalistic universe.

The *authoritarians*, on the other hand, see God as deeply involved in everything—so that whatever happens in life is certainly "God's will." Ours is not to reason why. God is in control. Good or bad, it's his call.

My own faith is not expressed in either of these positions. I can't be a thoroughgoing naturalist because of human uniqueness. If the world operated on naturalistic principles alone, matter and instinct would control everything. It would be a world on "automatic pilot," in which rational thought serves no purpose. The very fact that we are rational beings, however, introduces all kinds of possibilities that transcend pure materialism. With his/her mind, man chooses to build or destroy; to do good or evil; to love or hate; to have faith or un-faith; and, in many cases, to live or die. The mind of the human creature is *the* unique fact of life on planet Earth. If the source of that mind is God, as I believe, then it is at the point of our thinking, reasoning, brooding capacity that the natural order gets overlapped by the supernatural. This makes life far less automatic and predictable. But it means that instinct and matter do not have the final word on our existence. So we carry in our very beings evidence that life is more than naturalistic.

And, of course, in the coming of Jesus of Nazareth, God overlapped his creation in an unparalleled way. There he showed us what humanity—fully open to the Mind behind our minds—can be like.

So I'm not willing to rule God out of our lives and our circumstances. For similar reasons, however, neither can I swallow the authoritarianism that makes God responsible for everything that happens. The fact that our Creator gave us powers of thought and reason means that *we* exercise a lot of control over what happens in this world. God limits himself by giving us the freedom to think and to do. With that freedom go both *risk* and *opportunity*—and the loss of that is too high a price to pay for the elimination of all pain.

Thus, my sin, ignorance, complacency, and stupidity all help to determine whether life's pilgrimage is good or bad. If you made a list today of all the hurts you've known in the past two weeks (or years) that are directly attributable either to human choice or human ignorance, it would be a formidable list! My guess is that it would encompass most of the pain in your life. Now if you take Jesus' life seriously, you see right away that God's intention is for good, not evil. Confronted with disease, Jesus heals. Faced with grief, he comforts. Confronted with a storm, he stills it. If the life and work of Jesus afford us any gauges for measuring the intention of God, then neither suffering nor evil nor disaster is what God wants in this world.

But that only intensifies the problem!

It's obvious that this is a planet on which suffering, evil, and disaster often seem dominant. Jesus talked about God as a loving "Father" (two hundred seventy-five times in the New Testament that term refers to God). How can that match up with reality? How is that credible in the face of what is so obviously true about the human struggle.

Where is God when people hurt?

I think that an answer starts with an analysis . . . not of God, but of ourselves and what we know to be true about our human situation. If we can do theology "algebraically," calculating from the human-known to the divine-unknown, we may come to some understanding of God.

So, what are we?

We are biological creatures in a universe that seems to operate impartially and impersonally, and life is a mixture. Some of the things that give us the greatest joy may also give us great pain. *Our bodies*, for instance. Remarkable creations. I wouldn't want to be life-clothed in any other form. Yet there may be a microbe or a malignancy inside me as I write this that will take my life within six months—causing great pain and loss to my family. The *environment* is another good example. The same warmth and cold that make welcome the changing of the seasons, the same winds and tides that refresh us with mighty waves and gentle breezes . . . all have the capacity to do us harm. And our *relationships*—how precious they are. To share life-to-life intimacy, to be "of one blood" with all of humankind, enriches us tremendously. But our togetherness can become a threat when we depend upon an airline pilot, upon the driver of the car in the oncoming lane, or upon the packager of our food. All of them make daily choices about *our* safety.

The mix of life—celebration and grief—depends upon the operation of the cosmos *and* our personal choices. It's obvious that God has chosen to limit himself by the creation of both of those realities. The apostle Paul, in writing to the Romans, has a point of view on the dark side of nature that is worth considering. It views nature itself as being in bondage:

> For the creation waits with eager longing for the revealing of the sons of God; for the creation was subjected to futility, not of its own will, but by the will of him who subjected it in hope; because the creation itself will be set free from its bondage to decay and obtain the glorious liberty of the children of God. We know that the whole creation has been groaning in travail together until now. (Rom 8:19–22)

His perspective is that nature itself is "fallen" and in need of redemption. This understanding, which is thoroughly Jewish, was widely accepted in early Christianity as an attempt to explain the inexplicableness of nature's cruel wiles. I hve to confess that it makes a lot of sense because, although the cosmos seems systematic at times, there really is an ugly randomness at work at other times. In this particular passage, Paul goes on to say that God is at work to bring, not only humankind, but the whole created order into fullness. Someday a "new heaven and new earth" will complete that process just as our "resurrection bodies" will complete the process of redemption for us as individuals.

All of this leads me to two or three convictions about how God works with us. First of all, *God—though limited by his creation—works for redemption.* Some years ago, I heard a wonderful story by Dr. James Fowler of Emory University about a session he had with a twelve-year-old boy who had been reared in a family of atheists. His fifteen-year-old brother had a parrot that he named "God," and that was indicative of the ridicule that the divine name received in that family. The younger boy, David, believed in God, but he had a hard time holding onto his faith in such surroundings. Dr. Fowler asked David one day that if this God in whom he believed didn't exist, how the world might be different. The twelve-year-old thought a moment and then replied,

> It's like my aquarium; everything is supposed to be in balance - fish, water, seaweed, snails eating the waste, restoring oxygen and cleaning up the tank. But my aquarium is not in perfect balance. There are lots of times when I have to restore the balance. I think it's that way with God. We'll never know how much God actively *does* to keep the world working as well as it works.

God, though limited by creation (including us) *does* go on working for the redemption of all things.

There's a second thing that seems clear to me. *God does not force his will upon us.* "God's will?" A lot of explanations about why things are as they are have been buttressed by *that* simple phrase. My own understanding of God's will grows out of Romans 8: "We know that in everything God works for good with those who love him, who are called according to his purpose" (vs. 28). God's intention, that says, is always for good! That's "his will" for us and our world. Now you may want to speak of God's "permissive" will as allowing for pain and evil. That's all right, I suppose, but I'm not too comfortable with that. The word "will" to me says intention, choice, volition—and I feel strongly that pain and evil are not God's choice for us.

Even so, God doesn't force his will upon us—asserting himself, short-circuiting our freedom, brushing everything and everyone aside in pursuit of his ultimate purpose of good. So, Abraham lies, Moses murders, Jacob manipulates, David commits adultery, and Israel goes after other gods. God's response is not to give up, wipe them out, and start with someone else. Instead, he seems to stand back and say, "I won't force you. Let's see where your freedom will take you for good or ill." God doesn't coerce us.

Then, this other point: *God doesn't often take short cuts.* We do, if we can. We readily identify with Omar Khayyam:

> Ah Love, could thou and I with Fate conspire
> To grasp this Sorry Scheme of Things entire,
>   Would not we shatter it to bits—and then
> Re-mould it nearer to the Heart's Desire![2]

Fortunately, God isn't like us. He made a commitment to creation and to history and to process back at the beginning of time when he caused the world to be and called it good. Humanity entered the scene and messed up a lot of that goodness, so that now the goodness of creation becomes a goal and a hope. But God is committed to the process and flow of life and time . . . letting it last and letting it work.

Now there was a time when God showed us what a shortcut would look like . . . in the Incarnation. In Christ, God broke into the long-developing process to show us not only what redeemed humanity looks like, but to show us what the whole redeemed order of things will ultimately look like. C. S. Lewis makes this point in his book about the miracles of Jesus. Some of those miracles, Lewis says, are a speeding up of the process to demonstrate the coming order—changing water into wine, for example. We do it all the time. It just takes several months and years for that process to occur. Jesus did it more quickly. Feeding five thousand—we have the capacity to feed that many and more. It takes a year of planting, growing, and harvesting. Jesus reduced that to a matter of minutes. Other miracles, says Lewis, give us a glimpse into that future order where we'll finally see that the power of the spirit is greater than the power of the material: the raising of Lazarus, walking on the water, stilling the storm, for example.[3]

So, in Jesus, we get a foretaste of full redemption. Meanwhile, God trusts the process and allows it to work. He doesn't take many short cuts. At the same time, there are many Christian people who would gladly speak of miracles happening in their lives and of divine intervention. That's a faith-interpretation of reality, but it's very real to many people. I'm not discounting that at all. Nevertheless, the overpowering conclusion from the evidence at hand is that the process in which God works will make a certain amount of suffering and evil inevitable. Even accidental suffering is inevitable because it would take a steady stream of miracles to make it otherwise, and such shortcuts would undermine the probability of a predictable, dependable universe. Incidentally, they would also make faith one giant insurance policy . . . and that would ruin it.

As deeply as I believe all this, I'm still often uncomfortable with it. Quite often, my own faith-struggle lies in the tension between what I believe intellectually and what I feel emotionally. I know intellectually that God lets the process run, but I still get angry over tragedy. Emotionally, I'd like for God to run a tighter ship that doesn't allow for such painful deviation. I know better, intellectually and theologically. I realize that that would destroy a lot of my freedom, make life far less certain, and even detract from life's meaning. Still, I am chafed by natural disasters, angered by needless grief. Like Job, I have a running "lover's quarrel" with God over the suffering of this world. And like Job, I am not an outsider. I am God's child. We have a personal relationship, and God is able to handle my anger . . . my confusion . . . my doubt. God *is* a loving parent who allows my mixed-up feelings in the face of reality. He goes right on working, and he goes right on loving me.

In the final analysis then, what can I expect God to do in life's hurting times?

Two things, I believe. First of all, *God gets involved with us.* Paul says it well: "God goes on working for good in all things *with* those who love him . . ." Clearly, that means that we have a partner in the process of setting things straight! We have a fellow pilgrim in the process of redemption! Of course, the clearest example of God's commitment to be our partner was in Jesus' life and death, where he experienced all of the freedom and uncertainty of human life. It was God's most unmistakable way of getting into the trenches of everyday reality beside us.

But that was two thousand years ago; what good is that for the struggles of now?

If Jesus dies on that cross and his body still rests in that borrowed tomb, that question makes a valid point. But if in a way that we cannot yet fully fathom, Jesus Christ is risen and alive and in the midst of his people, that means he is *here now* struggling with us against pain and ignorance and sin . . . against all of those things in us and in the cosmos which keep his good will from being done! Even as God shares with us the responsibility for the way things are, he shares with us the commitment to help change them.

So, wherever and whenever the people of God struggle against suffering and evil, God struggles beside us. Not only does he say, "Let's see where your freedom will take you," but when that freedom leads to destructive dead-ends, he is in the arena with us saying, "We will stand before your Pilates, together we will die on your crosses, together we will empty your tombs." And this happens to Christians every day in the hospital room, the courtroom, the classroom, the board room, the work room. We look at the good in life and see in it, not mere coincidence, but the hand of God. We see human need and view it not as hopelessness, but as an opportunity for God to help and heal through us. Faced with humankind's cruelty and inhumanity, we see not fate, but sinful persons and structures standing both under God's judgment and in need of his renewing power. After all, Jesus himself told us to look for God in the struggle itself—among the hungry, the lonely, the naked, the sick, and the prisoner (Matt 25:35 f.).

God partners with his people because his love is a stubborn, dogged thing which will *not* be ultimately defeated! When people hurt . . . God stands beside us.

Also, *God shapes and creates us*. Paul speaks of the hope and the process of our full redemption in this way:

And . . . we ourselves who have the first fruits of the spirit groan inwardly as we wait for adoption as sons, the redemption of our bodies (Rom 8:23).

We are incomplete, immature . . . on our way to fullness and maturity. God can use the stuff of life—good and bad to help deal with that. He is a worker toward wholeness in us and in his created order. Though he does not send suffering, in a world that contains it, he may use its rough edges to bring deepening growth and perspective to our lives. Now we must be careful not to generalize the meaning of other people's pain, but I do believe

God will use the mix of life—even its negative parts—to go on shaping and creating us. After fifty years, I have learned that the mystery of God's love goes deeper than the mystery of our pain. That's a stubborn faith, but I have found it wiser than all our human rationalizing.

A woman who met a sudden and great sorrow exclaimed bitterly, "I wish I'd never been made." And a good friend responded, "You're not made yet; you're only *being* made—and this is the Maker's process."[4] Somehow we never begin to mature until we have faced life, not only at its best, but at its worst. There are some things we just cannot learn when everything goes smoothly and painlessly.

> I walked a mile with Pleasure:
> She chattered all the way,
> But left me none the wiser
> For all she had to say.
>
> I walked a mile with Sorrow;
> And ne'er a word said she.
> But, oh, the things I learned from her
> When Sorrow walked with me.[5]

A North Carolina friend told me that after Hurricane Hugo had left behind a trail of death and destruction in the fall of 1989, he and his neighbors had actually had to cut their way out of their neighborhood with chainsaws. After describing the utter devastation of that mammoth storm, he paused to say, "But in some ways our city is healthier now. We are more together, and our values are clearer."

Of course, you don't have to view trouble in this way. You can stay angry and bitter at what seems to be the mindless flow of life. But, if you are willing to be God's partner in the process of living—to give him your teachableness—you may find a maturity and a depth to living that you cannot know otherwise. "God goes on working for good *with* those love him, who are called according to his purpose," that is, with those who will take God as their partner in the learning process . . . those who will cooperate with him in the shaping and the deepening of life.

The problem of suffering and a loving God comes down, as most things do in Christian faith, to Jesus Christ. He came to reveal God's love, and he did. It was the best life that our kind has ever known, and it was crushed there on the tree. There was such promise and popularity in the early days of Jesus' ministry; then he died alone with but a handful of friends in the vicinity of his cross. It looked like utter failure. Yet within a brief span of time, the people most devastated by his death were pointing to that crucifixion as the greatest expression of God's love and power in all of history!

How did it happen?

It happened because they began to see that God could work toward the good of resurrection *through* the process of crucifixion . . . and he still *does*! That's why Paul can end this chapter in Romans by saying, "Nothing in all creation will be able to separate us from the love of God *in Christ Jesus our Lord* (vs. 39).

Several hundred years before the time of Christ, Aeschylus wrote Greek tragedy. In his play, *Agamemnon*, there are these potent words about spiritual healing: "Pain that cannot forget falls drop by drop upon the heart until, in our despair, comes wisdom through the awful grace of God." God's grace is amazing and marvelous, but sometimes it feels "awful" before it can become anything wonderful. As we travel from awful to wonderful, God shapes and creates us.

And while we are on that journey, there *is* Jesus Christ and his assurance that ours is a knowing, caring, and present God. Therein lies our hope . . . our faith . . . and our courage for the risks of daily living!

But what about "daily living"? Are we human types on this planet simply to survive . . . or might there be some deeper purpose in our existence?

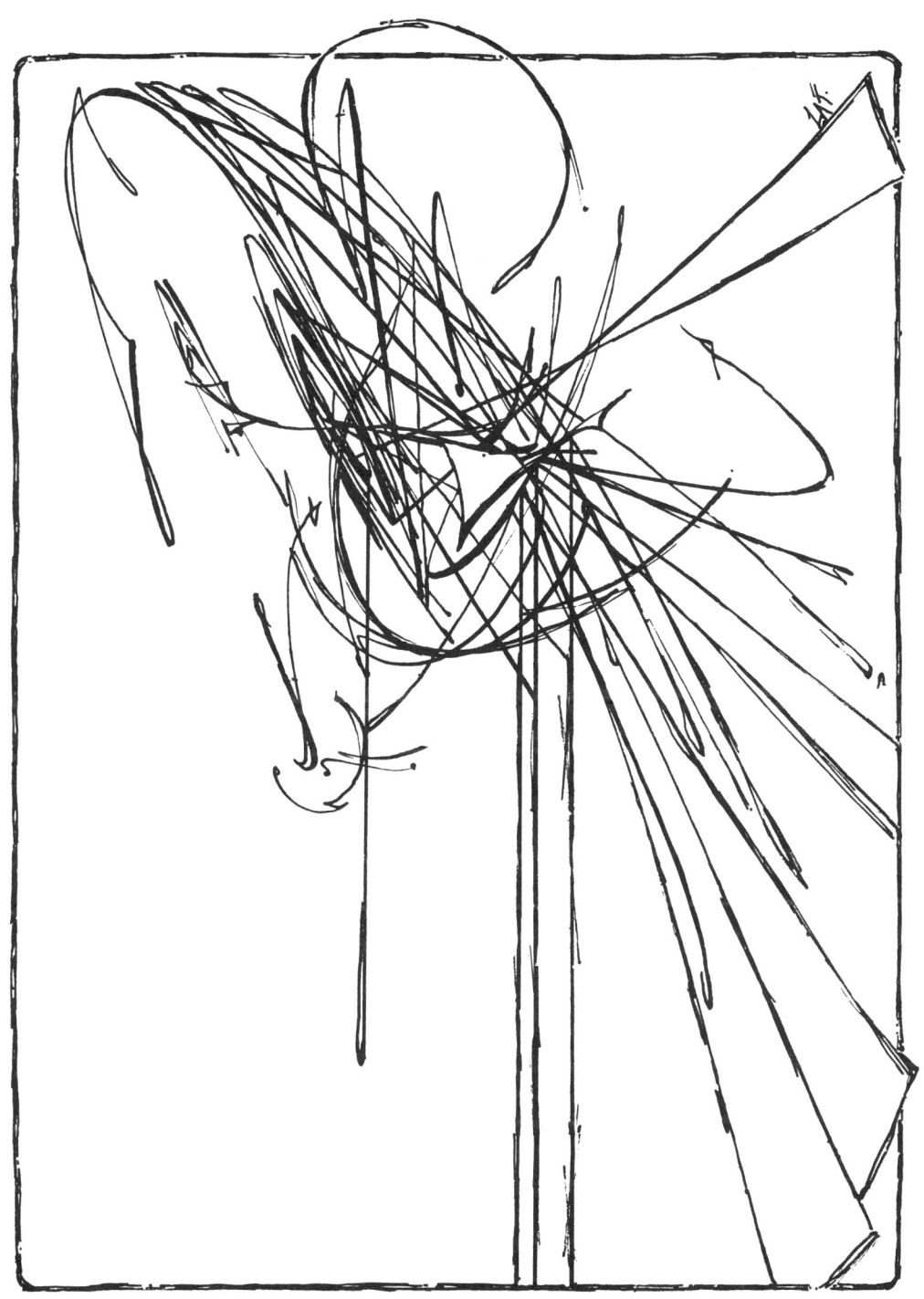

Chapter Four

"What Is the Meaning of Life?"

James 4:13-17

I read about a young woman who took a new job at a supermarket. First day on the job, a customer came in and asked for corn flakes. "Sorry, but we're out of corn flakes," the new sales clerk said. And the customer went off to another supermarket. The manager had seen it all, and he chastised his new employee, "Don't ever do that again. You should have said, 'Madam, we have no corn flakes, but we have Shredded Wheat, Rice Crispies, and All-Bran.'" The next customer asked for toilet paper, and as fate would have it, that was also out of stock. But the young lady dutifully said, "Sorry, madam, we have no toilet paper . . . but we have wallpaper . . . we have sandpaper . . . and we have confetti."

It's pretty difficult to substitute for some things!

On a little more serious note, one of those things that we seem unable to do without is meaning for our lives.

As I mentioned in Chapter One, the quest for meaning is not one we share with our fellow creatures in the plant and animal worlds; it's uniquely our own. Viktor Frankl (who, out of his death camp experience, developed a whole psychological system based on meaning) came to the conclusion that the *main* motivational force in humankind is the striving to find a purpose for one's existence. It's an illusive prey, and our failure to capture it can lead to the tragic wasting of life's resources. From my memory bank, I recall an assessment that says that lack of ultimate purpose has probably made more drunkards than thirst . . . more gamblers than avarice . . . and more suicides than despair.

To say, then, that the quest for meaning is a matter of life or death is not to overstate the case. It poses one of the enduring questions of our existence. Albert Einstein said that the person who sees his/her life as meaningless is not only unhappy, but scarcely fit for life. He also concluded that the only way to answer the question is to move into the territory of faith. We obviously need something upon which to base our existence, some lasting soil in which to plant our temporariness. You see, the world can't give us this. Matter doesn't explain itself; it's just there. If there's any meaning in it, we will have to look outside to find it.

Addressing this enduring question, the gospel of Jesus Christ has always stocked meaning as a main staple in its spiritual pantry. Jesus' *life*, we believe shows us what the abundant life he promised actually looks like in the flesh. His *death* reveals the love that God has toward us . . . a love that fixes our identity as those whose real destiny lies in relationship with God. His *resurrection* demonstrates the power and extent of the Father's love; it is so great that death does not defeat it. So you might say for the followers of Christ, meaning is not a matter of life and death; rather it is present in life and death . . . for all of our existence, we believe, is set firmly within the eternity and the care of God.

The book of James is one of those circular letters in the New Testament, written to address the needs of believers scattered all over the world. So naturally, it raises some of the universal human issues. "What is your life?" the writer asks, to which his first and most obvious answer is this: *Life Is perishable.*

That doesn't seem, at first glance, to be a very good way to major on the purpose of life.

> Come now, you who say, "Today or tomorrow we will go into such and such a town and spend a year there and trade and get gain"; whereas, you do not know about tomorrow. What is your life? For you are a mist that appears for a little time and then vanishes. Instead, you ought to say, "If the Lord wills, we shall live and we shall do this or that." As it is, you boast in your arrogance. All such boasting is evil. (vs. 13-16)

The context in this section of James is of possessions and wealth. These particular words are addressed to industrious businessmen and women who are planning future travel, sales, and profits. James does not condemn that, but he warns them not to get so absorbed in the "thingification" of life, that they see that alone as life's purpose. After all, there is the always deeper reality of dependence upon the Lord of life in whose hands are all things.

What arrogance to boast about tomorrow in the face of life's fragility!

Take a trip down into the mighty chasm that is the Grand Canyon, where each step may take you as much as 30,000 years back into geological time. Travel into the heart of the earth at Kentucky's Mammoth Cave and see the secrets stored there for perhaps millions of years. Compared to the age of our world, how brief is the life span of a human being! James is on target to describe life as "a mist which vanishes." It really is as brief and as tenuous as that.

It's obvious that the factor of life's perishability does not answer our question about purpose, but it *does* intensify our search for an answer. The very uncertainty of our earthly days breeds concern about their meaning. Nothing bestows value like scarcity, and the fact of death makes life scarce . . . hence, valuable . . . hence, the need for meaning. Confronted with the fleeting nature of existence, we humans seek meaning down a variety of roads.

For some, there's the road of *biological detachment*. "We are creatures of the earth who exist only to reproduce our kind before we die. It is our destiny to inhabit the world for a time, then disappear and make way for the next generation. Otherwise, it does not matter that we have lived." This view of life makes human existence pretty trivial—and pretty bleak. I remember reading that in several ancient Roman cemeteries the archeologists found numerous tombstones with seven letters inscribed on them. They discovered that those letters stood for a statement so familiar to the Romans that only the first letters had to be inscribed on the stones. The Latin words for which the letters stood said, "I was not. I was. I am not. I do not care." Existence as nothing more than a biological fact is evidently not new, but it's still not very satisfying.

On this road, people would tell you, "Don't take life too seriously. Don't invest much ego in a quest for purpose. Life's a cheat, anyhow; you're doomed to disappointment, sickness, aging, and death. Endure it, stir the pot, but don't load it up with any significant expectations." The modern stoics along this road of biological detachment would say to us, "Live, but just be cool. It doesn't matter."

At the other end of that spectrum is what I would call the road of *materialism*. On this road you will hear, "Taste all of life, regardless of the consequences. Life is scarce, so make the most of it. Grab the gusto. Eat, drink, and be merry. What you see is what you get . . . and want . . . and work for . . . and enjoy . . . and keep. I'm number one, and anybody else's back is just for climbing on—their needs being obviously secondary." Isaac Watts described this mindset long ago:

> There are a number of us who creep
> Into the world to eat and sleep
> And know no reason why we're born
> But only to consume the corn,
> Devour the cattle, flesh, and fish,
> And leave behind an empty dish.
> And if our tombstone, when we die,
> Be not taught to flatter and to lie
> There is nothing better can be said
> Than that he's eaten up all his bread,
> Drunk up his drink, and gone to bed.

This will be a crowded road on your quest for meaning, and a lot of Americans will keep you company. But in the deep places of life, the purely materialistic turns out to be the plainly mundane. It is the *superficiality* of life that haunts us as we travel this road.

Sitting in a hotel in Dallas in June of 1985, the week before Father's Day, I read a *Dallas Morning News* article that was based on an interview with the president of one of America's most prestigious department store chains. Five years earlier his daughter had asked him, "Daddy, are you happy?" Now forty years of age, he confessed that he'd never answered that question directly, although the words had haunted and driven him. "I can hear them still," he said, "as if they were hanging in the wind." He went on to talk about his blessings and the fact that his children were growing up. He also talked about being awakened in the night by disturbing thoughts that would not retire when he went to bed. He was unsure as to whether these disturbing thoughts were the result of stress at work. "They give me pause, in any case." He said, "They make me ask, in the face of a life dedicated to achievement, 'Is *this* all there is?'" Obviously, on the road of materialism, there comes a time (to remember Rabbi Harold Kushner's book title) when all you've ever wanted isn't enough.

If materialism and biological detachment don't provide meaning, what about the road of *happiness*? That's what we're looking for, isn't it? Isn't that the goal of human existence? Yes, we look for happiness in life. But, no, it cannot be the goal . . . because you don't get happiness by pursuing it. Happiness and unhappiness—both of which we will know in the course of a lifetime—are by-products. They are emotional responses to what is or is not happening to us.

So there has to be another road, a deeper reality in the quest for meaning. And indeed, there are other live options. *Work* gives meaning to many lives. It's the scaffolding that holds things together, and if you can't work (because of health or layoffs or retirement), there is, for a time at least, a real void in your life.

The discovery and understanding of *the self* offers meaning to many. "Who am I? What am I like? Will it matter that I have lived?" are questions of substance. And some would tell us that asking them repeatedly in the changing circumstances of our lives is the essential meaning of our existence. Here the quest itself becomes the goal.

So, when the writer of the book of James talks about the perishability of life, he intensifies and broadens our quest for meaning. "What is your life? It is a mist that appears for a little while and then vanishes." But that's only his first and most obvious answer. I think I hear in his words other answers now—strongly inferred, if not stated directly. Listen with me for a few moments.

"What is your life?"

It is *present* . . . a gift. Who among us asks to be born? Who bartered with the Creator for existence? Do we not live and move and have our being because a Creator has graced us with a wonderful gift . . . or is the life of woman/man fortuitous, incidental, and without direction? I choose grace.

These business people in James—traders and travelers—prepare to live and choose without any sense of the gift which is their lives. "If the Lord will, we shall live, and we shall do this or that" (vs. 15). Actually, that's a phrase straight out of paganism. The Greeks said it often: "If the gods will, etc." In fact, it was so common among them, it was virtually meaningless. The writer of James may well be saying to these people, "Don't ever view your life casually. It's never just a matter of trading and earning or of conventional religious by-words. Your life is a present from the Eternal, a precious gift handed you by the God of the cosmos."

And how special is the present! Your body has more than three million moving parts. Your brain has enough storage capacity to receive ten new facts every second, and five billion pieces of data may be locked in there by the time you're age five. (By age forty, there's room for fifteen trillion!) You are housed in the world's most sophisticated physical mechanism that is directed by the world's greatest computer! The fact is that there are billions of human energy carriers living on our planet at this very moment, yet no two of us are exactly the same. I believe that God gave you *your* life, and that gift confers uniqueness.

There is an old saying of the Hasidic Jews that a person should have two pockets into which he can reach at any time; in one pocket he/she should keep the words, "For my sake was the world created," and in the other, "I am dust and ashes." There *is* the perishability of life . . . but alongside that stands the importance of your/my *singularity!* Life is gift.

I sometimes think that we never stop to acknowledge this until we lose a life. I wish that you could stand beside me in the pulpit during memorial services and look into the faces I see. Somehow when we meet for those few minutes, away from the rat race, we come face-to-face with life's perishability and with the preciousness of this gift we've been given. We grieve the loss of those we love, but some of the somberness of such moments comes with the pause which remembers this remarkable present of being.

Your singularity bestows worth . . . you are somebody! It confers esteem . . . you are *imago dei*—no less than God's closest kin. And your singularity gives accountability . . . you are responsible, a trustee of the gift of life. Thus, a lasting purpose will scarcely come to your life or mine until we begin taking seriously our stewardship of life.

"What is your life?" It is a present from God.

It's also *partnership* . . . with other people, of course. But that's not the partnership James infers in our biblical text. His main point is that God is *not* a casual cliche . . . therefore, make plans for your life in partnership with God. That's a conscious choice, and no one else can make it for you—not your friends, not your family, not even God. God made you free, and you can walk away from him for a day or for a lifetime. You can seek meaning in other relationships or in your own personal resources, but I predict that you'll come up empty.

Wasn't it Sartre, the French existentialist, who concluded that a finite point (man) without an infinite reference point (God) becomes absurd and meaningless? Precisely! Unfortunately, Sartre could never bring himself to believe in God; he found it "very distressing that God does not exist." But suppose *you* can believe in God. And suppose you accept the validity of Sartre's point, namely, that God and human existence must be connected somehow for life to have meaning. Then to miss that connection, that partnership, is to miss life's meaning, is it not? The Bible's word for that is "sin"— not merely the do's and don'ts of moral behavior, but the basic choice to live without a relationship with God, personally chosen.

You see, I believe that Jesus of Nazareth came into this world to say to us human beings, "Don't put off partnership with the Father. Abundant life and forgiveness and purpose are here for you, if you will link your life to the One who gave it." The announcement of the possibility of that divine-human linkage is gospel (Good News), and there are a lot of us Christians who'll tell you that it really works. But you can push it aside and look for meaning elsewhere. Many people have and will.

Yet many of the voices of our time seem to be saying, "Without God, there's something missing." I'm intrigued by the fact that when Gail Sheehey wrote *Pathfinders*, her sequel to *Passages*, she found lots of average people who "just feel a dull hunger for a meaning at the core of their lives." And Collette Dowling in *The Cinderella Complex*, described a woman approaching forty, looking ahead to the emptiness of coming days "with a sense of something missing and overlooked." Bernard of Clairvaux, writing in the twelfth century, voiced our need succinctly:

> From the best bliss that earth imparts
> We turned unfilled to thee again.

Life is for partnership with God, and without that, our power, our money, our intellectual glitz, and our high-tech glitter will flounder in shallowness. Harry Emerson Fosdick called an earlier generation to this spiritual partnership by saying, "The deepest hell that some of us could fall into would be to have everything to live with and nothing to live for."[1]

"What is your life?" Perishable . . . present . . . partnership . . . and one other thing. It is *possibility.* The writer of James warns, "Whoever knows what is right to do and fails to do it, for him it is sin" (vs. 17). What is he saying? Just this, in part: "Don't sin by carving life up into separate categories of 'sacred and secular.' It's *all* sacred. To understand that is to acknowledge accountability . . . and to start living responsibly. Today/tomorrow, this place/that one, buying/selling, living/dying . . . *all* of your existence is shot through with the possibilities of God!"

And that's a great way to live! Everything you have or know or learn or do gets augmented by your partnership with God . . . so that your life becomes a channel through which grace, healing, reconciliation, and even strength can flow. This means that despite my weaknesses and my inconsistencies, God wants to work with me to do the kinds of things this world needs most.

> Life can never be dull again
> When once we've thrown our windows open wide
> And seen the mighty world which lies outside
> And whispered to ourselves this wondrous thing:
> "We're wanted for the business of the king!"[2]

For the Christian, life has infinite possibility in the world of here-and-now, as well as in that ampler existence which awaits beyond death.

I began this chapter by talking about meaning as an essential ingredient in the makeup of the human animal. I want to end on that note, as well. Karl Jung was the man who, from a psychological point of view, has taught us as much about the quest for purpose as anyone in the twentieth century. Analyzing his patients, Jung reached two very interesting conclusions. One was that meaninglessness is nothing less than the general sickness of our time, a disease that actually attacks our lives. His other conclusion was that in his patients who were past age thirty-five, the disease of meaninglessness was almost always due to the lack of a "religious outlook."

Meaningful living awaits meaningful believing.

Listen now, please, to that voice at the core of your life. The God who made you waits in love to begin filling your life with the rich purpose which he alone can give. All he needs to get started is your permission.

Deciding to begin the life of faith can be a pretty scary thing, however. Who knows how faith operates . . . or where it might lead? Let's take a closer look.

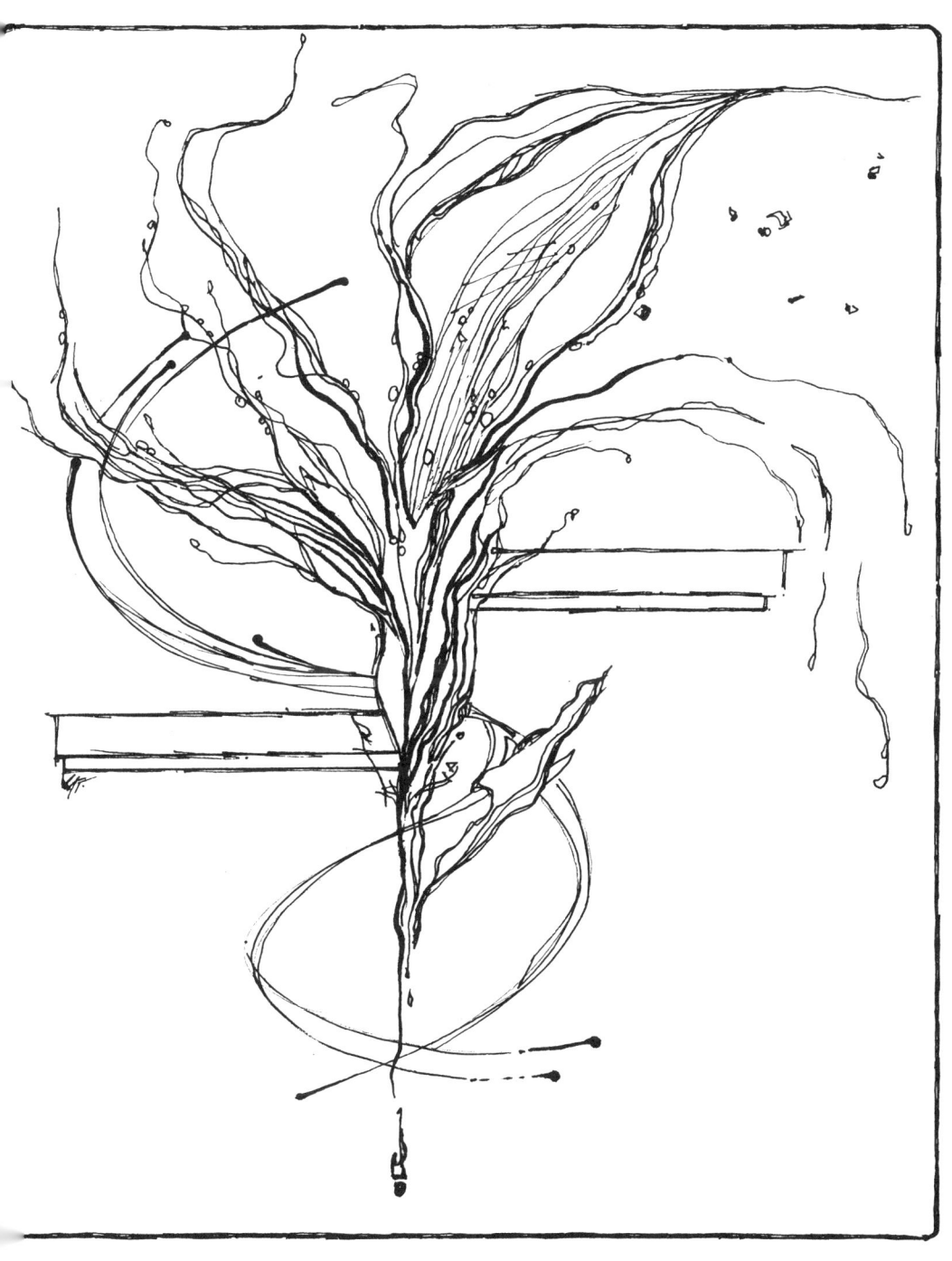

Chapter Five

"How Does Faith Work?"

Hebrews 11:1–13

A man collapsed on the floor of a department store. Bending over him, a minister asked, "Do you believe in God the Father, God the Son, and God the Holy Ghost?" The man on the floor managed to open one eye and say to the people standing around, "Here I am dying, and he's asking me riddles!"

I'm afraid that's the view of religion held by a lot of people. "I bring the deep lasting issues of my life to the church, and what do I get? Riddles, paradoxes, dogmatic formulas, and a ceaseless quibbling over proper vocabulary."

So what *is* faith? Does it work . . . and how? Are we talking about a game of theological scrabble here, or something that is a core reality of human existence?

In the book of Hebrews, we find one of the Bible's best known definitions of faith. It's not the only one. It may not be the best or the most complete definition. But it's certainly one of the most familiar:

> Now faith is the assurance of things hoped for, the conviction of things not seen. (Heb 11:1)

The word translated "assurance" means literally "things under" or "foundation." The word that is translated "conviction" means "evidence." According to this writer then, faith is building your life, not only on what you can see, but on what you cannot. It's a conviction about ultimate reality that says that behind the tangible and the obvious stuff of our existence there is the larger reality of God.

Our Hebrews writer continues:

> By faith we understand that the world was created by the word of God, so that what is seen was made out of things which do not appear. (vs. 3)

Then this:

> For whoever would draw near to God must believe that he exists and that he rewards those who seek him. (vs. 6b)

It's been wisely said that the problem with atheism is not that it leads to badness in human beings but to an incredible sadness and aloneness. Against that prospect of despair, faith raises the conviction that God *is* and that God *cares*. It's necessary to remember that "Creator" is a faith word, because to create something and to sustain it is an act of love . . . not an act of pure chance. According to this particular definition, God is also *knowable*—rewarder of "those who seek him." That assumes, then, the possibility of relationship and conscious friendship.

Now, this is not necessarily blind trust. I recall Archie Bunker's version of a Mark Twain saying: "Faith is believing what any fool knows ain't so." Not necessarily! Faith *may* begin in reason or in the obvious. Surely the God who gave us minds intended us to stretch them toward an understanding of their Creator. So, many early scientists saw their discoveries as ways of understanding how God runs the cosmos, and my own feeling is that modern science is truly our thinking of God's thoughts after him. Therefore, reason and observation, while they may or may not lead to faith, can build a bridge across the abyss of uncertainty and thereby open the path of possibility for faith. So you walk over the bridge of reason and nature and possibility, and you still have to decide about faith or un-faith.

But some people would say that the real question about faith is not what it is or how it works, but rather "does it matter?" and "who cares?" Faith in God, they feel is a monumental cop-out. Since humankind inhabits the earth, we should be able to cope with the needs of our occupancy without any help from the transcendent. In his final sentence of *Christianity and Naturalism*, Julian Huxley put it simply: "My faith is in the possibilities of man." It follows then that there's no need to put any stock in "things hoped for" or "not seen." The visible realities will do nicely, thank you. Our destiny is to live and struggle with them.

Others would say that faith in God in not so much a cop-out as a wash-out. They've been hurt and disappointed all too often. There is the lost job, the catastrophic illness, the injustice of society, the death of a friend. And whatever faith in God there used to be withered away before the hot blasts of reality's winds. Like the woman I knew in an early pastorate who confided to me on the day after we had buried her husband, and with anger rising in her voice, "I've always heard that you feel closest to God in terrible times . . . but I don't. I don't feel much of anything, but I certainly don't feel any nearness to God."

Writing from a concentration camp, historian Pieter Geyl described a cold and silent universe which goes resolutely on without end and without purpose. The possibility of faith is lost and will not return:

> The grace of God is gone.
> A vast indifference, deadlier than a curse,
> Chills our poor globe, which Heaven seemed to nurse
> So fondly. 'Twas God's rainbow when it shone,
> Until we searched. Now as we count and con
> Gusts of infinity, our hopes disperse. . . .
> God is dead;
> And the sanctuary of man's heart is empty,
> A void place through which blows a bitter wind,
> Rustling the worn leaves of a lost beauty,
> Stirring the barren twigs of a vanished peace.[1]

But the need for faith refuses to die. We may talk about the cop-outs of belief and the possibilities of our humanness, but the truth is that on our own, we haven't done too well. Human history is as marked by our greed as by our greatness . . . by the darkness of our wars as by the splendors of our technology. If there *is* strength and forgiveness from beyond us, we still need it.

The washout of faith in the face of life's pain and uncertainty usually springs as much from our misunderstanding of faith as from anything else. God is not a fairy-godmother, and faith is not three wishes. Evil is not the will of God, and Jesus' life tells us that

God's intent is for good. If there is real support and clarity from beyond us, we still need it. The hunger for faith remains.

Lofton Hudson used to say that the circumstances of life will usually lead us either to a sense of futility or to a saving faith. Suppose you choose faith instead of futility—or at least you think you want to choose faith. How does it happen? And how does faith work?

This eleventh chapter of Hebrews deals with faith in God as a center or core out of which we may live. It's based on God as Creator, but mostly it's based on the understanding of God as *redeemer*—one who comes to us in Jesus Christ, in history and in love, to forgive our sin and to equip us for our best humanity. (In Chapter Twelve, the Hebrews writer calls Jesus the one who pioneers and completes our faith by his death and resurrection.) Most of chapter eleven is given to a listing of people who did center their lives in God by faith. I like the idea of centering as synonymous with faith. *Credo*, Latin for "faith" or "belief," literally means "I rest my heart upon." To live by faith is to rest your heart upon God . . . to let down the weight of your life upon God . . . to center your existence in God. How does that happen?

The model of Abraham, one of those listed in the eleventh chapter of Hebrews, is a good one. Let me zero in on it and try to get at how faith works in our lives. First of all, Abraham's model says that *you make a choice.* There are a lot of things over which we have little or no control in life.

Several years ago, I ran across a tongue-in-cheek saying that goes,

> Except that I inherited certain characteristics from an unknown number of unknown ancestors, was deeply influenced by persons, most of whom were dead before I was born, and shaped by circumstances over which I had no control, I am a self-made man.

I also recall the story of the man who bragged about being a self-made man, and his friend's response was, "You should have asked for some help!" We need occasional reminders of our finitude and of our interdependence. But we also need to remember that we *are* responsible for our lives and the choices that we make, within the framework which our history bestows.

Faith is one of those things in life that must be chosen. I can verbalize and write about what my faith means to *me*, but finally you much choose personal relationship with God for yourself—otherwise, it lacks integrity and vitality. Søren Kierkegaard, so insistent that the Christian faith of his own day be personally chosen, wrote that to try to make our religion anyone else's without requiring them to go through whatever is necessary to make it their own is, in fact, to deprive them of their relationship with God. Abraham learned that truth:

> By faith Abraham obeyed when he was called to go out to a place which he was to receive as an inheritance; and he went out, not knowing where he was to go. (vs. 8)

In the world of Abraham, personal faith in God was not the only option open to him. As a young man, he lived in Ur of the Chaldees, center of one of the most advanced civilizations of that ancient time. Apparently, Ur was a place where education was highly valued, where philosophy and art flourished. Religion was popular, too, with chapels all over town for the worship of various gods. Abraham and his family likely worshiped many different deities, and in that, the struggles of young Abraham's soul may have begun.

Maybe it was the gods—perhaps they seemed so temporary, so cruel and whimsical, so limited that Abraham yearned for an ultimacy which they could not provide. That's a pretty good description of the surrogate gods many of us worship here in the nineties—the gods of power or money or status. They can disappear in an instant and leave us still longing for something more lasting.

There's an imaginary story about God's task of fashioning man and woman. One of heaven's hosts overlooking the process is alarmed. "But you're giving this creature freedom," he says. He'll never be wise enough or strong enough to handle it. He will think himself a god, will boast of self-sufficiency. How can you risk it? How can you gamble that this creature will ever return to you? And God replies, "I have left him unfinished within. I have left in this creature deep needs—a homesickness which only *I* can satisfy. . . ."[2] Abraham may have known some of that homesickness.

Or maybe it was the restlessness. Abraham and his family were part of the *'Apiru*, the nomads and wanderers of this era. They didn't stay in Ur very long, and as they proposed to go on to Haran and Egypt and beyond, that may have precipitated the crisis of faith. The local gods of Ur won't do in Haran. On the journey of life, we need a God big enough to travel through all kinds of territory, *not* the provincial gods of one time and place and culture.

So, somewhere in his mind and soul, a young Abraham decided to bet his life on the call of a greater God. He was surely not the first to be called by God, but he may have been the first to hear . . . and to respond. So he moved from a comfortable, secure life out into the unknown, because he believed that God had some purpose for his life.

That's the call of faith that comes to every one of us. In the midst of all the competing claims for loyalty and in the face of your limited human options, the God who created you and who loves you calls you to follow. Best of all, in Jesus Christ he extends to you a very human hand to lift you up and to point the way. He has a great purpose for your life in fellowship with him . . . but you much choose to have it. And if you make that choice, like Abraham you will find support for all parts of the journey.

> I would rather walk in the dark with him
> Than walk alone in the light.
> I would rather walk by faith in him
> Than walk alone by sight.

Like any ongoing relationship, you will not have full knowledge and complete answers at the outset. Marriage, friendship, and parent-child relationships are all areas of faith where an early choice must await further light. But there must be a beginning! How does faith work? You make a choice.

Then, *you start a pilgrimage.* "By faith," we read, "Abraham sojourned in the land of promise as in a foreign land, living in tents . . . " (vs. 9a). One of the things you quickly learn about faith is that it's a *growing* center for your life. Abraham didn't have much real estate, and the real estate he'd been promised was in somebody else's hands, so he kept moving. And things were in constant transition.

If faith in God is going to mean anything, it will have to stretch and grow. If you'd asked Abraham to describe God at the different junctures of his life—Ur, Haran, Egypt, Canaan—I suspect he would have done it differently each time. This would occur, not because God changed, but because Abraham's perception of God and of himself as God's person changed greatly. Faith is a growing center. When you head out onto new trails, when you leave Ur behind, when you grow up, you have to decide what to leave behind and what to carry with you.

And it's not always easy, this pilgrimage of faith. In the twelfth chapter of Genesis, Abraham makes his covenant with God, a great promise to serve him. Then, right on the heels of it, he stumbles into Egypt . . . tries to lie his way out of a tough spot . . . and all but forgets the promises of God for his life. The circumstances of life make it not only hard to understand God, but to have faith. And as you read the story of Abraham in Genesis, you discover that he was openly skeptical of God at times. When Dostoevsky said, "My hosanna has passed through whirlwinds of doubt," he could have been speaking for Abraham . . . and for many of us as well.

All of which means that faith in God is for real human beings, not puppets or robots or stereotypical "saints." Faith is living *through* the tough times into deepening and changing, because you believe that God will be faithful to you as you traverse the shifting sands of an earthly journey.

One destination of this faith pilgrimage is spiritual maturity, and I'm reminded of those now familiar words of philosopher Alfred North Whitehead—that spiritual maturity comes to us as we move from God as enemy . . . to God as void . . . to God as friend. Choosing to live by faith in Jesus Christ is to affirm that the God of this universe is not enemy or void, but friend.

The Christian faith believes that "when the Word became flesh and dwelt among us," it was God's most personal and direct way of extending friendship. Because I believe that, it helps me get through some difficult days on my spiritual pilgrimage. Nevertheless, there are seasons of disappointment and despair, when I find Whitehead's cycle repeating itself. I experience anger and conflict in my relationship with God. I feel a void in the midst of

God's seeming silence. Only later does the warmth of friendship return. What I try to remember during such times is that in any true friendship, there *will* be conflict, and there will be periods of silence and separation. But neither conflict nor silence necessarily means the loss of the friendship. And my faith is that *God stays* even on those days when the warmth of favorable circumstances or the goosebumps of a spiritual "high" have gone.

Rachel Carson awakened a generation of us with her 1962 book, *Silent Spring,* where she attacked the irresponsible use of pesticides, talked about the balance of nature, and pushed us into a fresh awareness of ecology. A decade earlier, however, she wrote *The Sea Around Us,* where she described the fascinating life that goes on beneath the waves. She told us about plankton, the vegetation that is food for the smallest creatures of the ocean. The word means "drifting," or "wandering." And plankton travels thousands of miles, pushed to and fro only by the change in currents of the great oceans.

Analagous to that, I believe that faith in God is pilgrimage and *not* plankton. You may travel far on the inward and the outward journey, but your roots are secure in the faithfulness of God. "Come and begin," he says "Go and I will go with you." You make a choice and you start a pilgrimage. Faith works that way.

One other thing, namely, *you travel with a family.* That's extremely important, because sometimes we tend to see biblical characters as isolated individuals and super-heroes. Faith does begin with a personal decision. But it gets reinforced, clarified, and interpreted as we travel with other pilgrims who are on the same journey. The Hebrews writer says that Abraham lived "in tents with Isaac and Jacob, heirs with him of the same promise" (vs. 9).

Abraham shared his tent with a family. That's a pretty good working definition of the church—the family we share the tent with, the people we travel with, those who are "heirs of the same promise," the people of God. We need a faith-family, some flesh and blood with whom to grow and change. For that reason, I never feel apologetic about asking people to join our church while they're in Houston. I believe in Christianity as personal commitment to God as we know him in Jesus Christ, but I also believe that it's absolutely essential to have a family, a community of faith in which that life center gets nourished and strengthened.

In Chapter Nine, we'll talk about the church in more detail, but let me recall with you Robert Raines' parable of the crab; I think it's appropriate here. These hearty crustaceans must live pretty long lives because they change shells a lot in the process. The shell in which they die is probably not the first one they grew, but as they adapt and grow, one shell is sloughed off, and another one begins to grow. Of course, it's in the times between the shells that they are the most vulnerable.

Raines suggests that our faith is like that. There are times when old certainties give way, and new convictions are just beginning to form. Perhaps it's a fresh and disturbing understanding of God. Maybe it's an emerging aspect of self-awareness. Or it could be the scary prospect of trying to serve God in some new way. It's during these times when the shells change, when faith is in flux, that we're expecially vulnerable and we need a family. During such uncertain days, when uncertainty is turning into change, we need to share the tent with our Isaacs and Jacobs. The biblical model is clear from Genesis to Revelation: we travel with a family, and the life of faith is strengthened.

So how does faith work? You make a choice . . . you start a pilgrimage . . . you travel with a family. There's a lot more to faith than this simple formula, but I think that these *are* the basic ingredients.

Leslie Weatherhead recalls a story from Denmark—an old fable about a spider. The spider slid down a single filament of web from the lofty timbers of a barn and established himself on the lower level of rafters. There he constructed his web, caught flies, grew sleek, and prospered. One afternoon, wandering about his premises, he saw again the single thread that stretched up into the dark above him and thought, "How useless." He snapped it. Whereupon his web collapsed, and his whole world came crashing down![3]

You can live without God, severing any conscious ties with the Eternal. You can choose un-faith as a center for your life. But in so doing, you may be forgetting one of the most important things about human existence . . . that faith in God ties us to that

Ultimate Reality without which if life does not collapse, at the very least, it languishes for lack of a lasting center.

Faith works . . . but only if you're willing to have it.

Chapter Six

"But Aren't Saviors for Weaklings?"

John 4:39–43

Many years ago when he was University Preacher at Harvard, George Buttrick invited his friend, Archibald MacLeish—poet and writer—to participate in worship leadership at the university. MacLeish was clear and somewhat abrupt in refusing. Later in the afternoon, he phoned Buttrick to apologize for his abruptness and to explain that he couldn't accept the invitation in good conscience. Buttrick said he understood and let it go. But that night the preacher's phone rang again, and MacLeish said, "Hello, George? This is Archie. I'll do it. But one thing must be clear. I'm not convinced that Christianity has the answers we're looking for, but I do think it has the right questions."[1]

At this halfway point of our journey through some of life's ongoing questions, I hope that you, dear reader, are beginning to share that opinion. I hope it's obvious to you that in the struggle to believe, we Christians really do wrestle with life's essential stuff, even when we don't deal with it very well. Allowing for the foibles and foul-ups of very human believers, I would still contend that personal faith is the best resource we have when we begin looking for answers and for direction.

Certainly one of the things that belongs to our humanity is the issue we face in this chapter, namely, "How do we handle our failures?"

There's a labeling mentality in the modern marketplace that I really deplore. We like *winners*; we don't like *losers*. "She's a real winner" . . . "Boy, is he a loser" are sentiments which turn my stomach. Failure is the unpardonable sin of those in the know, and mostly it has to do with a skewed picture of success. If I don't make a certain level of income, if I don't hold a certain kind of job, if my duds don't contain a certain label, and above all, if I'm not moving up the right ladder, I'm not "successful."

So many of our clues we take from expectations outside us, foisted onto us by who-knows-who, and we quickly buy into them because there's a hollowness inside us where our spiritual centers ought to be. So, when we lose, when we fail to measure up, we become guilty of not playing the game or the role well. These are shallow failures, and they must be dealt with mostly at the level of our false expectations and our faulty goals.

But there are deeper ruptures in life as well. Our sins (whether we use that term or not) are real—against God, against each other, against the earth and the air and the human family . . . including ourselves. South African writer Alan Paton felt the anguish of it: "There is a wound in the creation, and it groans and travails until now, and I don't know why."[2] In a memorable poem which he wrote during Christmas of 1947, my friend and teacher, John Carlton, described eloquently the ongoing brokenness of our world:

> The scourging breath
> Of poisonous guns has withered fields—once
>   meadows fair
> . . . . O God, we sense amid this festive
>   Yuletide air
> Sin that haunts our waking hours and turns our
>   dreams to dust.

What's to be done? Various voices in today's world would tell us, "Saviors are for weaklings; I'll make it on my own. I grant you that life is a steady struggle, but don't insult my intelligence or my integrity by introducing some sort of messiah into it." A lot of these stubborn souls would agree with the conclusion of H. L. Mencken that God is no more than "the immemorial refuge of the incompetent, the helpless, the miserable."

One of the ways we deal with our sins and failures is to become philosophical about them. "I'm in charge of my life; my destiny is in my hands. No outside help needed."

The assumption is that religion would dehumanize us by becoming an escape hatch from responsibility. "Forgiveness," said George Bernard Shaw, "is a beggar's refuge; we must pay our debts." And, at a 1989 conference, cable television magnate Ted Turner labeled Christianity "a religion for losers" and added, "I don't want anybody to die for me."

This is a popular way to handle failure—evasion by philosophy or spurious theology. If you look at the story of Jesus and the Samaritan woman found in the fourth chapter of John, you'll see that just as quickly as Jesus calls attention to the series of marriage and family failures that this woman has experienced, she tries to shift the discussion to a theological exercise: "I think you're a prophet," she says. "Let's discuss the proper precincts for liturgical exercises." That didn't work with Jesus. It won't work now. Philosophize all you want about ritual or logic or human responsibility; there's still a mystery of evil and of human failure that refuses to fit all our categories and our formulas.

Sometimes we pass the buck as a way of handling guilt. "It wasn't me," he said in the garden, "it was this woman you gave me." And she said, "The snake's the culprit" (cf. Gen 3:12—3). "I don't know what happened, Moses, it was the people's idea. We threw all this gold into the fire, and out jumped this golden calf," said Aaron (cf. Exod 32:23–24). "It's not my fault" . . . all the way from Nuremburg to Vietnam and beyond . . . "I was simply following orders."

Of course, a lot of us deal with our sins and failures by denial. We get busy . . . we stay on the go . . . we entertain and get entertained at the rate of 100 billion dollars a year in America. Lois Cheney described this syndrome:

> Feeling blue . . . buy some clothes.
> Feeling lonely . . . turn on the radio.
> Feeling despondent . . . read a funny book.
> Feeling bored . . . watch TV.
> Feeling empty . . . eat a sundae.
> Feeling worthless . . . clean the house.
> Feeling sad . . . tell a joke.

Ain't this modern age wonderful? You don't gotta feel nothing. There's a substitute for everythin'!

God have mercy on us![3]

Buried under an avalanche of stuff and schedule, however, our failures do not seem to die. Instead, they get resurrected as neuroses or psychoses or despair . . . or compulsion . . . or addiction. I don't think it's honest to generalize about a complex problem, but with drug use at epidemic levels in our country just now, I was struck by what Louise Bernikow said in her book, *Alone in America*. It's a study of loneliness in our society (including the considerable values of solitude), and the author makes the observation that a lot of drug use in our culture is specifically related to loneliness. What I wonder about is how much of the loneliness and estrangement in our country relates to our inability to handle our failure. We deny it and cover it up and pass the buck—maybe fearful that if people knew us and our sins, they wouldn't like us or want us. So it's easier not to risk it . . . and denial may lead to addiction. I don't know, but my hunch is that there is some linkage.

I remember a young man who appeared in the office outside my study a couple of days after we had buried his grandfather. Apparently, his grandfather's death had precipitated a need in his life, and he'd come to the pastor to confess that need. He told me about being on drugs, and I asked him to tell me what it was like. "Oh, it's wonderful," he said. "A lot of us get together, do the drugs, get high together, and it feels terrific." "But what happens," I wanted to know, "when the high wears off and the drugs leave your system?" "Oh, nothing happens," he said. "We just go our separate ways and live our lives until the next time." Their comradeship was fed by the artificial. It was counterfeit *Koinonia* and short-lived . . . fellowship leaning on a crutch. The need for acceptance, community, and understanding, despite our failures, is so very strong that we may try to get it any way we can . . . artificially, if necessary.

Here's what it comes down to. The difference between Christians and non-Christians is not the difference between the sinless and the sinners or between the weak and the strong. We *all* sin and fail. We Christians bleed with the same humanity as everybody else. The big difference is that we have found a way of dealing with our sins and failures that brings healing instead of further fracturing. In fact, biblical words like savior and salvation carry in themselves the concept of healing . . . of being restored to wholeness, and I count more than sixty different references in the Bible which use words like "forgive," "forgiven," or "forgiveness." That says overwhelmingly that there are spiritual resources for the handling of our sin and guilt and that the prospect of restoration is a very strong one.

At the same time that the Bible is very big on personal accountability for our lives and our choices, then, it's also quite clear about our need for outside help in the healing process. The Hebrew scriptures are unanimous in their opinion that God (Yahweh) is Savior. In the New Testament, God is called Savior many times, as well. But in the Magnificat of Mary, where she acknowledges "my soul rejoices in God my Savior," the clear promise to her is of One-to-come who will "save his people from their sins." So Jesus is born, and his very name means "Yahweh saves." In practical terms, it's about the same as the word "savior" itself,

Maybe that's why the Gospels don't call Jesus Savior very often. His very name means that, and they don't have to. Here in the fourth chapter of John's Gospel, however, we find one of those rare references to Jesus as "the Savior of the world" (vs. 42). When this Gospel was being written, that phrase was almost always given to the Roman emperor. But somehow, these Samaritans knew better. After two days with Jesus, their assessment is, "We know that this man truly is the Savior of the world."

What convinced them?

I think they were persuaded by the same things that convinced the woman at the well. They are those qualities in Jesus as Savior that will heal us if we will give him a chance to deal with our failures.

One of the things that identified Jesus as Savior to this woman, and to her brother and sister Samaritans, was his *affirmation* of her. She came to the well at noon, even though the usual time for drawing water was at dusk. She came at noon, perhaps, to be alone and to escape the separating stares of others. Here she is, and here is Jesus, and to her amazement, he engages her in conversation. An old morning prayer of ancient Jews thanked God that one was born neither a woman nor a Gentile. She was both, yet this strange man crosses those barriers to inquire about her life. That says to her, "You're worth talking to. You're worth spending time with. You are not worth-less. You are a God-send."

The healing of a life begins with the affirmation that there is personal worth there, despite personal brokenness. I recall a Houston Metropolitan Ministries video that detailed the various ministries of that fine social service agency. In it was a short vignette about an older woman, a Meals-on-Wheels recipient. She told how the volunteers stopping by regularly cheered her up, even though they didn't have time to visit. Their brief stop, she said, "makes me feel like I'm not throwed away." During a brief visit on a Samaritan well curb, Jesus says to *this* throwaway life, "There's living water for you. God's grace can make you whole. You are not trapped in your past or your present." Jesus affirmed her, which means he accepted her time and value and friendship right where she was. And as the story reveals, she found in that affirmation the strength to begin a new life.

The gospel is *not* "shape-up/straighten out and God will love you." The gospel starts with Jesus' affirmation of your value . . . and of your possibility. As you receive and internalize such love, you find the strength to change. I don't remember now where I first heard it or read it, but it has been well said that human worth is not the result of salvation, it is the *reason* for it . . . and the reason that hell is such tragedy.

They play verbal games for a few moments, Jesus and this woman, until he says, "Go get your husband." Then she confessed her sins. She admitted that she had failed in the most intimate relationships of her life. Five times, she had been either vixen or victim, and now she had settled for a tarnished "shacking-up" with another. She was cut off from her community, estranged by her broken promises. But Jesus knew her story . . . and he was willing to help.

"Come see a man who told me everything I ever did," she said to her friends back in town. And you have to believe that those friends may've been outcasts, too, since *she* counted them as friends. "Come see a man who saw through me and all my defenses and my excuses . . . a man who saw more than the shame and the guilt, who saw *me* as a worthy recipient of living water."

Someone said once that conscience is that still small voice that makes us feel still smaller. My guess is that this woman felt pretty small when she came to the well that day, but Jesus' affirmation of her generated in her a larger and healthier self-understanding. She was not a nobody, a nothing, a failure, despite the fact that she must have seen herself that way. It took Jesus to change her mind, and in his affirmation of her were the seeds of her salvation.

In the same vein, Luke's well-known story of the prodigal son reports Jesus' saying that when the son was heading home, covered with guilt and self-loathing, "while he was still a long way off, his father saw him and felt compassion for him and ran and embraced him and kissed him" (Luke 15:20). His father saw him . . . not the rags nor the dirt nor the poverty nor the smell nor the shame. His father saw him . . . not the bum nor the drop-out nor the drunk nor the addict. Salvation begins in knowing and believing that God sees in us not merely what we have done or haven't done, but who we can be as full members of his family. If God sees us that way, maybe, with his help, we can start believing it, too. And that, my friend, might just change your life!

Jesus' sensitivity to this woman's need got him a hearing with some other Samaritans, much to the chagrin of the disciples who were traveling with him. So the second quality about Jesus the Savior that emerges in this story is his *action* on behalf of her and her friends. I doubt that this woman's life would have been changed significantly if Jesus had finished his conversation at the wellside and returned to his northbound road. She might have told her friends about her conversation with this unusual man, but it would have become little more than a fond and faded memory for them. "He spoke of living water, of grace and forgiveness, of a new life for us. Those are nice words, but they don't mean anything now."

So Jesus didn't leave it to his words. He acted. He chose to stop on his journey and spend two days with these people, probably staying in their homes, sharing their lives. And when he left, the villagers said to the woman, "You were right. We have seen and heard for ourselves. Now we know that this is the Savior of the world."

There would come a day later on in his ministry, when Jesus would act in an even more decisive way. His love would face its sternest challenge in Jerusalem in the form of a traitor's kiss, a Roman procurator's cop-out, and a deadly cross on a hillside. The question with which he would struggle in a garden would be the same he faced here in a Samaritan village. In the village, the question was, "Do you care enough to stay with a group of despised, discouraged Samaritans for two days?" There in Jerusalem, the question would be, "Do you care enough about people to die, rather than renounce the kind of ministry that accepts and forgives in the face of human sin?" You see, it was such incidents as this one with this unnamed woman that helped string him up at Calvary. An unfettered love is usually called on either to back down or to die. Thus the New Testament writers looked at his cross, and they called him Savior. More and more in the writings of the apostle Paul, the death of Jesus becomes the great saving act of God on our behalf. "But God demonstrates his own love toward us," Paul writes to the Christians in Rome "in that while we were yet sinners, Christ died for us" (Rom 5:8).

It is the total thrust of *his life*, however, which gives meaning to his death. Jesus did not die to *become* our Savior; but precisely because he *was* and *is* our Savior, he chose to die. His action, in giving himself to a handful of Samaritan villagers or to the whole world on a crucifying hillside is the strong intervention we humans need to help break the cycle and the power of our sin.

In Arthur Miller's play, *After the Fall*, we meet a man named Quentin. Defensive and up tight, he quarrels with his wife, he qualifies most of his statements, he has an incessant need to be right. Then one day he asks himself why he has this driving compulsion to always justify himself. His answer is that he's lived his life as if there were some sort of judge on a bench always watching him and his failures. Liberation comes to Quentin when he's finally able to believe that the bench is empty and that there is no one to judge him.[4]

The good news of Christianity is not that the bench is empty, but that the judge who sits there is also "Savior." We do live in accountability to one who knows our actions and our needs, but that One who judges us is not an angry tyrant. He is a God who acts in love to rescue and reshape us. He takes upon himself our form, our humanity in the man from Nazareth. And even when it means the cross, he acts to redeem us. In deeply moving words, Austin Farrer describes his encounter with the Savior:

> God forgives me, for he takes my head between his hands and turns my face to his to make me smile at him. And though I struggle and hurt those hands—for they are human, though divine, human and scarred with nails—though I hurt them, they do not let go until he has smiled me into smiling. And that is the forgiveness of God.[5]

"Saviors are for weaklings?"

I don't think so. Still, every person I know has to deal with his or her failure to be whole somehow. Whether you do that on your own or not is up to you. But if you seek what this Samaritan woman was seeking—affirmation, sensitivity, and healing—come to Jesus. For the Samaritans were right, "This is indeed the Savior of the world."

But wait a minute! This "sin" business is confusing. Isn't that term so narrow, so quaint even, as to be irrelevant for handling modern problems? Let's take a look.

Chapter Seven

"Haven't We Outgrown Sin?"

Ephesians 4:17–24

Paul Tournier, Swiss doctor and counselor, on the twentieth-century mindset:

> People no longer want to know about good and evil. . . . In the place of strict principles, we have psychological explanations. Sin is rejected as one of those outworn ideas which in a century of intelligence ought to be dead and buried.[1]

Decades earlier, British physicist Sir Oliver Lodge had already concluded that modern man "is not worrying about his sins." And I recall seeing a copy of *Life* magazine from the mid-forties. It was a December issue, and one "letter to the editor" writer lamented the seeming irrelevance of a Christmas gospel of forgiveness for a society that had no real sense of sin.

Now, in the marketplace of the nineties, the beat goes on, "Everything is relative . . . including morality. Go with the flow and don't sweat it."

> Never knowing where we're going,
> We can never go astray.

So, does anybody believe in sin anymore? Haven't we outgrown that old-fashioned idea? I don't hear this particular question raised in very direct fashion these days, but it is an ongoing query behind that lurks an overwhelmingly negative attitude on the part of our society toward any serious consideration of moral behavior. In his book, *A Nation of Strangers*, Vance Packard reported the conclusions of a thirty-year-old salesman living in a highly mobile neighborhood where he knew none of his neighbors, who said, "There's no morality here, and I guess it's because nobody knows anybody, so that you can get away with stuff you couldn't in the old days where everybody knew everybody and what they were doing." There it is—ethics by consensus or peer pressure, but *not* by individual choice.

Yet, evil rears its head in all those myriad places where lives are snuffed out, trampled on, and jerked around by ugly reality. But somehow, unless it's got a technological/scientific solution, a lot of us moderns don't count it as a legitimate problem. That's the secularization of the modern mind. "Evil exists, yes, of course, but give us a little more time, a few more generations, and we'll deal with it. Our old genetic patterns or our cultural institutions can be altered. If we can enlighten the mind and feed the body and change the social surroundings, we can solve the problems of evil and immorality."

I grant you that economic and psychological problems are real, and the impact of our know-how can be very good and powerful in dealing with them . . . yet somehow, *man* is amiss! Man—in all genders and colors and sizes and cultures—is amiss! In the past fifty years, human achievement has surpassed anything the world has known before. The splitting of the atom, the probing of space, the wonders of medical research, the explosion of communication technology—none of that is to be minimized.

But there's a spiritual vacuum and a basic need that, unmet, warps us . . . so that our expertise often spawns instruments of devastation, and our technology often creates distance and loneliness. In the face of all our human prowess, all our knowledge (to remember the words of Thomas á Kempis) "is not without some darkness."

During an early period of spiritual searching, the intention of C. S. Lewis, the noted Oxford don, was to bring his life completely into harmony with what he called the universal Spirit. As he looked seriously within for the first time, however, he reports "There I found what appalled me: a zoo of lusts, a bedlam of ambitions, a nursery of fears, a harem of fondled hatreds. My name was Legion."[2]

In the face of any evidence—personal or corporate—for the existence of sin, I continue to hear dissenting voices that say, "Let's don't talk about sin, please. That's a dated term from an earlier era, and it's so limited. Everybody's outgrown it by now, except for the church, and you know the church's way of talking to itself in its own private jargon. In the real world, sin has no place in the modern equation. It just doesn't fit."

Some of the negative reaction toward any serious discussion of morality in the modern marketplace is directly related to our failures in the Church. Often, we've been over-eager to catalog and condemn, rather than to major on the good news of forgiveness. Our preaching and teaching are often perceived as being stronger on guilt than on grace.

At other times, our treatment of sin has been out of balance in another way—speaking loudly and specifically on selected moral issues while ignoring larger ones. Usually, we evangelical Christians have been hard on privatized morality, while failing to make much connection with larger social issues. The churches of my childhood, for instance, were down on dancing and "dirty" movies and drinking. But they were strangely silent on race relations, human rights, war, and anti-semitism.

I was a seminary student from Alabama in 1961 when the executive secretary of our state Baptist convention came to speak to the Alabama club at our school. The early sixties were days of racial upheaval in Alabama and throughout the south, and church people found themselves in a real crisis of integrity. One of our faculty advisors asked this denominational servant what these men and women from Alabama could expect to say and do about this issue if they returned to Alabama Baptist pulpits. His quick response was, "That's a social issue. We keep it out of the pulpit, and we just preach the gospel." It was at that point that I began to realize that "social issue" was a euphemism for a lot of things that mattered! The church was becoming adept at ducking them, while sticking to its own narrowed, individualistic ethos. Studying the book of Acts during those critical days, I concluded that personal ethics and social concerns, far from being opposites or mutually exclusive of each other, are in reality two sides of the same moral coin.

Of course, one of organized religion's most obvious weaknesses is that we often treat sin as somebody else's problem. Either you're a sinner or a Christian—an outsider or an insider. On the inside, saved and snug, we don't worry too much about sin because we're victorious and cheerful, and we've got it together. A lot of our talk about sin is past tense, before conversion, and there's not much honesty about the real struggles of right now. I once heard Keith Miller say that many Christians are great taxidermists. We drag out our old sins like we would an owl or a hawk that we've stuffed and defanged and now can look at and talk about safely . . . when what we really need to do is open the window and let a live one fly in and deal with that!

Augustine warned us centuries ago that we should never fight evil as if it arose totally outside ourselves. We Christian believers know that, yet the world reads our perfectionistic tendencies otherwise. Therefore, those outside the circle of faith decide that either we aren't human enough to have any validity, or that we are very human and we pretend not to be. Either way, that's phony, and who needs it?

Admittedly, we church folks have mishandled the subject of human sin. At the same time, we *didn't* invent it. It's there in the human fabric from day one of our time on this planet. We've simply given a name to and a sometimes faulty interpretation of this obvious facet of the human dilemma.

One of the positive things about the Church's understanding of sin is our insistence that our sin is all tied up with our accountability. We can thank Moses and the prophets, John the Baptist and Jesus for this timely reminder. We are not the powerless pawns of fate, the helpless victims of history. Our decisions can shape history. Our choices enable us to take responsibility for our lives. So this burden of accountability, heavy though it is at times, is far better than being harassed and clobbered by unbending inevitability. "Original sin" is but a classic theological term which describes our human penchant for making wrong choices. So strong is this tendency that it seems imbedded in the human racial consciousness. In *East of Eden*, John Steinbeck confessed, "We have only one story. All novels, all poetry are built on the never-ending contest in ourselves of good and evil."

To speak of sin, then, is to speak of one of the best documented facts in the marketplace of the nineties: obscene violence, irresponsible sex, dishonesty, theft, graft, and addiction. Sin breaks out in ghettos and on Wall Street, both in our greedy hearts and in our holocausts. Among the intelligentsia and the plain folk of our time, I hear a growing awareness that despite the considerable progress fueled by our human genius, somehow *we* need fixing.

During a Houston lecture two years ago, Scott Peck, physician and author, confided to his audience that one of the things that drew him to the Christian faith was the Christian understanding of sin . . . that we *do* miss the mark, that we cannot *not* be sinners, that we *are* in need of forgiveness and cleansing. I recall also that shortly after World War II, English philosopher C. E. M. Joad, militant critic of things religious, astounded many people by professing Christian faith and joining the Anglican Church. A major attraction, he said, was that the Christian understanding of sin made more sense of life's darker side than any other explanation.

So, for all of our euphemisms and our synonyms, we seem to be stuck with sin. We all need fixing in one way or another. Let me offer a very modest contribution to the ongoing dialogue by discussing briefly how to define sin and how to deal with it. Of course, the credibility of church people like me is inextricably tied to a willingness to be confessional about one's own needs. So, please understand that sin is my problem, too, and that I write to you as one struggler to another.

How do you *define* sin? Writing to the Ephesians, Paul urges them to review their own spiritual experience, and he helps us toward a definition:

> You were taught with regard to your former way of life to put off your old self, which is being corrupted by its deceitful desires to be made new in the attitude of your minds and to put on the new self, created to be like God in true righteousness and holiness. (4:22-24)

At our core, there's a self that is off-track, and a new self is needed. It's more than a matter of keeping rules or moral codes—it's deeper than that—it's down deep where we choose the direction for our living.

There's a key phrase in verse 18 of this same chapter—"separated from the life of God." Bottom line, *that's* what wrong with us humans! The fallout is graphically described in the words of this Ephesian passage: futility, deceitfulness, insensitivity, impurity.

God created you for the wholeness of life that can only come from fellowship with him. Full life and personhood are tied up in that relationship. It isn't God who moved away from such kinship; it's us. And we seem to do that by either opposing or giving up on God's purpose for our lives. To oppose that purpose means that I bump God and enshrine self as "the Master of my fate, the Captain of my soul." The temptation is not necessarily to be bad, but to be God. Somehow, when we start out playing God, we wind up acting like the devil. Berdyaev was right that nothing is so terrible as humanity when there ceases to be anything above it. Hence, the damage of our "old self" choices is scattered across the landscapes of history.

But we may just as easily give up on God's purposes for our lives. We drift away. We choose, not reaction, but inaction. As the Genesis story suggests, we let the snake or some other tempter call the shots and avoid taking any personal responsibility. With William Temple, we may feel, "The trouble is that I can be good if I want to, but I don't want to."

In either event, we are alienated "from the life of God." And that's our core problem. To turn away from God is to lose ourselves and to lose our way in this world. You see, though the Bible does give a lot of press to specific acts of sin, they are always set within this larger context, namely, that a relationship with God has been broken, and evil things get done as a result.

In the Hebrew language, the Ten Commandments are actually ten short phrases of two words apiece, and our word decalogue means, literally, "ten words." So that famous passage in Exodus is sort of a pocket-sized reminder of the larger context in which we live our lives, namely, our relationship to God and to those around us. When the former is out of focus, the latter gets contaminated. Far from being a private and wholly negative set of propositions, the Ten Commandments were given to a community, a group of ex-slaves on their way to becoming a society. Hence, the decalogue attempts to express for all the people how covenant with God looks "on the hoof" . . . in daily life and in corporate responsibility.

My Baptist brother, Walter Rauschenbusch, long ago insisted that sin is never a private transaction between the sinner and God. "Humanity," he contended, "always crowds the audience room when God holds court." The destructive effect of human sin grows and intensifies as it feeds on our politics, our economics, and our religion. Our sin deepens into demonic darkness with our genocide, our racism, and our greed.

And of course, the Bible is very democratic in describing sin . . . the big word throughout is ALL. When Alexander the Great sat for a portrait, it is said that he always insisted on turning a particular profile to the artist, never full face. For on the other cheek was an ugly jagged scar, indicating that he, too, the master military strategist, had known the sting of the sword as surely as had any ordinary warrior. All of us bear the scars of sin upon our lives. It's part of the human mortgage that perpetually falls due in us and around us . . . there are no exceptions.

So, how do we *deal* with sin? Not by denial, that's for sure. In Ephesians, Paul talks about people who are "darkened in their understanding" and who are trapped "in the futility of their thinking" (4:17–18). For them, reality is covered up, denied, ignored.

Leslie Weatherhead recalled how, on a bitterly cold day, a great golden eagle spotted a carcass floating down the Niagara River. The eagle left his perch on the high cliffs, circled around and down, dug his talons into the body, and began to assuage his hunger. After a while, the great bird began to realize that he was nearing the place where the water dropped over the falls, but thinking he was free to rise whenever he wanted to, continued to eat. Just as the carcass got to the edge of the falls, the eagle spread his wings to fly away . . . but he could not! His feet were frozen into the body, and he was taken over the edge to his death. All the time, the eagle had been thinking, "I'm free to fly away," and all the time he was becoming more and more captive.[3] The refusal to face our need, the failure to acknowledge the tenacity of sin, the denial of our need . . . there is no solution for sin there.

Also, you don't deal with sin effectively by personal idealism or hard work or more stringent moral intentions. I meet people fairly often who try to deal with a guilty conscience by stepping up the pace of activity. "Works salvation" is how an earlier Christian generation described it, and this attempt to justify ourselves can be a strong motivator. We may be, as Coleridge wrote:

> Like one, that on a lonesome road
> Doth walk in fear and dread,
> And having once turned round, walks on,
> And turns no more his head;
> Because he knows a frightful fiend
> Doth close behind him tread.[4]

Often, hand in hand with this "trying harder" attempt at salvation, goes a deep-seated fear of God as an extension of the fear and power of the guilty conscience. So that when the ledger is out of balance and our positive deeds do not outweigh our sins, we worry about the results, especially when the threats and troubles of life overtake us.

On October 23, 1989, in nearby Pasadena, Texas, a Phillips Petroleum plastics plant exploded, killing twenty-three people. A few days after, one man who escaped was quoted in the local newspaper as saying, "You'd better believe I'll be in church this Sunday." Now, I wouldn't minimize any impetus toward God in a time of tragedy, and I experienced that particular tragedy at close range, since I happened to be preaching in a Pasadena church that very week. But I do wonder if the explosion caught one man, at least, with his ledger out of balance.

Since the rootage of sin lies in our separation from God, however, it's clear that ending that separation will *not* come with feverish effort. We can never do enough. There's just no way to measure up in all ways, and at all times.

So, it's a gift—this end of alienation, this salvation from sin, this peace that you seek. It comes to you packaged as the grace of God that alone can forgive and restore your life. In Ephesians, Paul says that it is not just matter of "putting off" an old self, it's a matter of "putting on" a new self. Maybe the most important thing he says in this text about this new self is that it is "created to be like God in true righteousness and holiness" (vs. 24). And that's a great choice of a verb! This means that freedom from the guilt of sin is not something we can do for ourselves; it is something *created* and *bestowed* by Another. The God who freely chose to create us in the beginning now chooses to recreate us, and he does this as we "come to know Christ" (vs. 20).

How does Christ help?

Well, he's as human as can be in his tears over his city, Jerusalem, and his friend Lazarus . . . in his laughter at parties and his chuckles in the parables . . . in his anger when religious people objected to his helping a man with a withered hand (and at least a couple of other times) . . . in his tenderness with blind Bartimaeus, with the woman who washed his feet, with the disciples more than once . . . in his fear when, in Gethsemene, he confesses that he'd just as soon not do the most loving thing in the world. Jesus helps because he's one of us!

He also understands our spiritual needs. He understands our overdose of ego—like the Pharisees—or our lack of ego—like the woman taken in adultery. He knows our tendency to live out of a self-center and deny any need for help outside that. In his own earthly lifetime, Jesus saw our human willingness to take the things of God and exploit them for personal profit without much consideration for others around us. He knows how we live as if *our* feelings and *our* wants are all that matter. Paul said to the Corinthians that though Jesus was without sin, he was certainly tempted in every way as we are tempted. That helps because it means that Jesus not only knows us, but that he knows our darkness and our deep need. So this is the One who lives, dies, and is raised among us. This is the One sent by God, who comes to lift us toward our best humanity.

The word on dealing with our sin is a word of grace. It is not about rules or codes or balancing the books, but it's about restored relationships and new life. It's a word about the kind of God who seeks out men and women in love and forgiveness.

One of my favorite stories is an old C. Roy Angell account of a boy who came home to lunch one day to tell his dad that the fish were biting in the mill pond. "All the boys are going fishing after school this afternoon. May I go?" he asked. His dad said, "I'm sorry son, but we're planting corn today, and you've got to plant the beans." But the boy was persistent. "If I finish up, can I go then?" His father smiled and said, "Yes, when you plant all the beans in the bucket, you may go." You can imagine what happened. The boy flew home from school that day, grabbed his bean bucket, and took off for the bottom land. He went along the first two or three rows at a trot, dropping two beans in each hill, just as his father had directed. But he noticed that the beans weren't disappearing from his bucket very fast, so he began to throw handfuls in each hill. Finally, he just dumped what was left in one last hill and went fishing. He promptly forgot about the beans until one later afternoon when his dad said, "Let's walk down and see how the corn and beans are turning out." The first few rows looked fine. The next few were much too thick. And finally, the spot where he'd dumped the bucket was covered in beans, beans, beans. Instead of giving him a thrashing, his father put his arm around his shoulder and said, "Let's kneel down here. I want to talk to God." The boy would never forget that prayer: "Father in heaven, I don't mind loosing a crop of beans, if you'll just teach my boy that the beans always come up in life. Teach him that he will always reap what he sows."

God is the kind of father who comes to the bean patches of my life and yours. He sees the mess we've made of things and the judgment we deserve because of it. Yet he falls down beside us in the person of Jesus Christ, and he says to us something like this: "I cannot keep you from all the consequences of your sin—the crop comes up. But I can forgive you and give you strength to go on from here."

That's how the Bible says we can deal with our sin.
That's grace.
That's salvation.
That's the beginning of restoration to health and wholeness.

"Haven't We Outgrown Sin?" 87

"Fine," you say, "I'm beginning to get the picture about personal faith. But you preachers are always pushing the church as something neat and necessary. To be honest, institutionalized religion leaves me cold. If I forget the church, the faith-struggle gets easier."

Well, let's think about that.

Chapter Eight
"So Who Needs the Church?"

Acts 2:41-47

It was July 4, 1986, a Friday morning. Attending a summer seminar at Princeton Theological Seminary, I had been jogging on the university stadium track, and I was walking back to my hotel. The university was beautiful in the early morning haze and light. Its great Gothic structures hovered over me as I walked through a deserted campus. A few hundred yards from the chapel, I paused and looked back at it—one of the most beautiful among many magnificent buildings. It was then I learned that I was not the only person up and out early on an holiday morning. A man who looked to be in his sixties walked out of the front door of the chapel, took off his glasses, blew his nose, turned and looked at the structure he'd just departed, stood in silence for a moment, then walked away. We didn't speak, since I was some distance away and he didn't see me.

But surrounded by the silence of that early morning and long after he'd walked away from Princeton Chapel, I stood and wondered what he was doing there. Was he a former student? Was he there because of the Fourth of July? Had he lost someone in a war? Was he there to give thanks? Had he come to remember or perhaps to forget?

Why do people go to church?

Fifty million of us do in America on any given Sunday. A recent study shows that, in my denomination, fifty percent of all active Southern Baptists drive at least five miles to church on Sunday. South Main Baptist Church in Houston has been my pastorate since 1985, and there fifty-three percent of us commute at least ten miles to Sunday worship. Thirty-four percent of us drive more than twenty miles. Why? What's the attraction? I think it has to be more than activism, because most of us have other places to go and other things to do. It has to be more than escapism; there are other ways to run and hide from the rigors of life in the fast lane. It could be habit or convention that takes us to church, but those things are scarcely able to sustain attendance for very long.

The whole phenomenon of church membership and church attendance in the United States is a fascinating one. One of the reactionary cries of the 1960s was against institutional religion. "The church is dead. Bury it, and leave it." Of course, to have a good funeral, you've got to have a willing corpse, and the church was unwilling to die. In fact, over these past two decades, by some standards the church in America has made a modest comeback.

Still, there is skepticism and uncertainty. "Who needs the church?"

It's a good question in light of several present day realities. American civil religion, for one. To the question, "What is America?" British writer G. K. Chesterton once replied that it is "a nation with the soul of a church." He was describing a kind of national creed—a national dogma—which is, for lack of a better term, religious. Chesterton and others have long since uncovered an American way of life that blends God and nationalism. It's a merger of religious and political ideals that touches many of our national institutions—a religion in general, a national faith in a God-to-whom-it-may-concern. Some readers may recall President Eisenhower's famous statement from the fifties: "Our government makes no sense unless it is founded in a deeply felt religious faith—and I don't care what it is."

In a country with a wide pluralism of faiths and with separation of church and state, American civil religion seems to meet a need for some sort of national consensus. A nation with the soul of a church, a civil piety as part of the American way of life. That would seem to undermine, if not eliminate the necessity of organized religion and institutional churches.

Also, there seems to be in America a growing group that has been described as "believers, but not belongers." In their recent survey, *American Mainline Religion*, Root and McKinney concluded that two main things characterize American religion over the past thirty years—privatism and pluralism. A heavy dose of individuality, blended with the freedom to proliferate new organizations, gives American Christianity a quality unique in the world, namely, an ever-growing list of denominations. If the religion of colonial America was largely monolithic, structured, and public, an awful lot of today's religious fervor appears to be diverse, fragmented, and private. In *Habits of the Heart,* Robert Bellah and his associates interviewed a young nurse who described her faith in these words:

> I believe in God. I'm not a religious fanatic. I can't remember the last time I went to church. My faith has carried me a long way. It's Sheilaism—just my own little voice.[1]

So . . . who needs the church?

A third factor is the rampant secularism of the modern age. Humankind, we are told with great regularity, has come of age, and what many of our forebears looked to God to provide we can now do for ourselves. We provide irrigation more than we pray for rain. We wonder about the stars and confidently expect NASA to soon enable us to wander among them. We control the rate at which our kind multiplies, the environment in which we live, and to some extent, the health and length of our lives. To many Americans, a transcendent deity now seems irrelevant. Therefore, any affiliation with a community of faith would seem unnecessary.

Still, the church survives. Millions join and get involved. Billions of revenue dollars are generated (if American religion were a company, it would be number five on the Fortune 500 list, ranking just ahead of GE and just behind IBM). In many communities across the nation, the church and its ministry remain central in the lives of its adherents.

Part of the answer to our question about the church would seem to lie in the obvious spiritual hunger of today's marketplace. Martin Marty calls us a nation of "metaphysical shoplifters" and "spiritual window-shoppers." The evidence is plentiful. Horoscopes are read religiously. Meditation is encouraged and done in the workplace. Psychic phenomena are explored. The new age movement encourages us to find the deity within us and change the world. All of this is happening in a culture where secularism is supposed to be the order of the day.

There remains among us a stubborn need for some conscious connectedness to God. There's a heavy residue of yearning for a linkage with that Source who lies beyond all our mortal and material stuff. A year ago I read an interview with one of modern Russias foremost poets, Andrei Voznessensky. As he looked at life in the twenty-first century, he projected that the great Russian contribution during that era will be in matters of the spirit. That shouldn't be too surprising, he said, because though they stopped religion in the Soviet Union, the spiritual needs have remained.[2] With or without *glasnost* and *perestroika*, that kind of assessment is quite interesting . . . and, I think, understandable.

Alongside this interest in things spiritual, however, there is in most human cultures a dislike or distrust of organized religion. "I'm religious, but I don't need the church" is the attitude. The rationale may be, "The church is too fanatical, and I don't want to be identified with that," or "Institutionalism kills the fervor of warm personal faith. Who needs it?" Or, I sometimes hear this: "I tried the church as a child when they forced me to go. I didn't like it then, and I don't need it now." Other voices say that the church is too lax, makes no demands, and is consequently a waste of time. Or this: "The church is tied to the past; we need a contemporary word." And, of course, the old favorite, "Religion is a private affair. It's what you do with your solitude. 'My God and I go through the fields together and down the road and on into the sunset. So, who needs the church?"

How, then, shall we speak for the church—those of us who are committed to it? My initial answer is . . . softly and with few words. We always do better to let our *living* do the speaking. It's a painful admission to say that the church at times is a cliché-ridden institution that sounds irrelevant to its time . . . or a narrow-gauged crowd where fierce idealism easily leads to cruel fanaticism . . . or a broad fellowship that is eager to sell its soul to whatever is current in modern culture.

But as we struggle for answers to our questions about the church, I think there is some help in the book of Acts. There we meet the church at its earliest, the first blush of a Christian faith-community. These first church folks were flawed and inconsistent followers, as are we. In fact, a lot of our New Testament got written specifically to address the conflicts and the ignorance of these early churches. But even with their "feet of clay," they walked through some pretty remarkable times. Acts Chapter Two says that plain old people began to sell possessions and use the money to feed and clothe and house others, so that a thing they would later call ministry started to happen. It also says that they broke bread and praised God. Between table and temple, something they would later know as worship and liturgy started to form.

It all seems to have grown out of two basic realities. First, there is a *story*. Verse 42 says that they "devoted themselves to the apostles' teaching." We're not told at this point what that teaching was, but if you look at the apostles' preaching throughout the book of Acts, you find that it is a story, a strong memory about God as Creator and Deliverer and Savior, who now sends Jesus to call us back to himself. "God has made this Jesus . . . both Lord and Messiah" (vs. 36). So the story is that the great God who made all that is is a seeking God who loves us and comes after us and overtakes us and forgives us and saves us to be what we should be. In today's spiritual context, where God may seem intellectually respectable, but strangely silent, we tell the story that one day in a life, on a cross, and at a forsaken grave, the very word of life itself was spoken by God . . . through Jesus . . . for every person. Acts 2 says that on the day of Pentecost, three thousand people decided to open their lives to that word and that story, chose to receive, not an intellectual argument or a doctrinal abstract, but a personal experience with the God who reveals himself in Jesus.

What is the church? Its a bunch given birth by that story. We've heard it . . . we've believed it . . . we've bought it. Now it shapes our very lives. So when we preach and teach and share the gospel of Jesus Christ, the church is attempting to meet the most basic need of humankind—the need for relationship with God.

When I urge a man or woman to receive Jesus Christ as personal Savior, I'm urging him/her to find the core purpose of human existence. Nothing could be more relevant than that. And when we forget to be sharers of the story, we forget a very basic ingredient in being church.

My good friend and mentor, Findley Edge, tells about a visit to New York City. He was studying a church there that had a reputation for bridging the gap between the church and the world. He visited one of the members, a middle-aged woman, in her apartment and asked for her perspective on the church. They talked about community concern and the church's considerable social ministry. But after they'd talked for a while, she exploded, "The church has lied to us!" Findley was taken aback and could only ask what she meant. "I mean," she said, "that the church told us that our problem was poor housing and lack of education and low wages, and we *do* have those problems. But those are not our basic problems . . . our basic problem is *within us*."[3] For all its flaws and faults, the church still holds aloft the beacon of personal salvation and new direction for every human life. On our best days, we're carriers of the story . . . of good news . . . of fresh possibility.

It's often on people's worst days that they're most ready to listen to the story . . . when the shallow answers won't answer life's deepest questions anymore, and when all the other roads that seem to lead to real meaning have become dead ends, and when—feeling pain or discouragement—there's an ache to be with somebody who knows this story of inclusive grace.

A friend of mine who's a social worker placed a five-year-old child with some foster parents. The parents were church-goers, so they took the little girl to church the following Sunday, furnishing her with twenty-five cents for the offering plate. My friend stopped by the house after church to see how things were going in the foster family, and she found the child somewhat angry and upset. When she asked what was wrong, the little girl said, "That woman (her foster mother) told me we were going down to God's house and I was to give him this quarter. Well, we went and I looked all over the place, but I never did find him!" To a five-year-old, everything, including God, can be distressingly concrete. But God *is* present, to young and old, in the telling and re-telling of the story of love and salvation. The church believes that story and bears it to those around us.

"So Who Needs the Church?"

The other thing present here in the book of Acts is a *people*. Once three thousand people had bought into the story and others were being added to their numbers daily, one of the most critical needs facing the early church was for a community. The strongest argument for the church is what happens *after* someone hears the story and believes. It's important to remember that Jesus' Great Commission (Matthew 28:19-20) calls on us not to make converts, but to make disciples. What happens after conversion is that you begin to think *theologically* about life and all that touches it.

> So shall no part of day or night
> From sacredness be free;
> But all my life in every step
> Be fellowship with thee.

"Now that I am a believer in Jesus Christ, what does that mean in terms of my time, my money, my influence, my lifestyle, my loyalties? How does my faith shape my values?" The church can help you answer those questions because it's where persons are being shaped into nothing less than the likeness of Jesus Christ. The cultural, political, racial, and class values out of which we have been operating we bring along with us into Christian discipleship. And we do not grow easily or rapidly away from domination by those and into Christ-likeness. But in the faith-community, alongside other believers, we slowly start that change-process. We begin to *think* theologically . . . and to *act* intentionally.

You see, wholeness and reshaping of life always happen best with other people. One's experience with God *is* very personal, but the expansion and the expression of it are very corporate.

Recently, I heard Myron Madden relate a delightful experience hed had as chaplain at a New Orleans hospital. He was visiting a new mother and, in the course of the conversation, asked her the name of her new baby. Without hesitation, the woman answered, "We've decided to name our daughter I Am Christian—I Am Christian Tucker." "That's an unusual name," said the chaplain. "I don't believe I've heard it before." "I know," the mother said, "but there are so many people out in the world who don't know who they are; we've decided to give our daughter a head start." A few days later when Myron saw the new father on a crowded elevator, he wondered what English grammarians in the crowd thought when he asked the question, "How is I Am?"

A "head start" is fine. Any child's understanding of herself/himself will not be found in a vacuum, however, but *in relationships* with people, with family, with a community. Just so, conversion to Christ may bestow upon us a lifelong identity, but it is within the believing community, led by the Holy Spirit, that that identity gets clarified and interpreted.

Thus it is to that spiritual family that I turn and return for the strengthening and the stretching of my life. It is there that I find family in the midst of my loneliness. It is there that I am being molded into what the story promises . . . a new creation.

It is also among the people of this spiritual family that I will often find comfort and strength. On one of his frequent visits to the States, I heard Bishop Desmond Tutu tell about the hope and reassurance that people of faith in South Africa were experiencing during very difficult times. I was particularly struck by his account of a village prayer meeting that went late into the night. Already shops, churches, and houses had been destroyed, and many of the people in the prayer meeting were going to be forced to leave the following day. As they gathered for prayer, one man whose house was to be demolished within hours, began his prayer with the words, "God, we thank you for loving us." Somehow that simple, deep affirmation of faith became a source of nourishment for an embattled community on its knees.

Sometimes in the church we are people who can answer each other's questions, sometimes we can help clarify one another's fuzziness about faith, and sometimes we can just be present for each other. There is an adequacy in common tears that is sometimes better than all the logic in the world. The Spirit of God is in them . . . and with his people.

One other thing about the people who are given birth by the story, namely, we're people on mission in the world. The same Spirit of God who shapes us in prayer and in community calls us to serve in the marketplace. From day one, the book of Acts says that the church was busy telling the story, giving, healing, reconciling, and ministering. The gospel of Jesus Christ speaks a redemptive personal word but has within it profound social imperatives as well.

Though it happened nearly twenty years ago now, the stinging, biting truth of this story lingers with me. A group of activists interrupted a Sunday morning worship service in a midwestern Methodist church. Their demands were read to the congregation and the warning given that if the demands were not met the following week, they would see to it that the church was filled with thieves, prostitutes, drug addicts, and alcoholics. The remarkable assumption was that the influx of people with such obvious spiritual and emotional needs would be perceived by the church as *a threat*—the feeling being that the *real* business of the church is something other than contact with such people and their needs.

What a terrible misunderstanding of the nature and the mission of the church! The God of the church has not embraced the saving of souls to the exclusion of justice and reconciliation. The division between sacred and secular is our creation, not God's. So for God's people, certain things always go together: God's love and the hurt in our world, spiritual concern and physical need, personal faith and social ministry. Now, we won't all agree on where to grab hold or how to grab hold, and we don't have to. One body, many members. One spirit, many gifts. Diversity is the New Testament pattern. The Holy Spirit equips us for both the structuring and the doing of our mission—as individuals, as networkers, or as a church body.

So, who needs the church? When I hear that question, I think of the spiritually satisfying, intellectually stimulating, risk taking life that I have found by belonging to the people of God in Jesus Christ. I recall with Albert Schweitzer that Jesus comes to each of us as he did to those first Galilean followers. He calls us to follow, and it is only as we follow and walk with him where he leads that we begin to understand him, ourselves, and our world.

I cannot imagine that journey without a faith-community. In truth, I cannot imagine even trying to *live* without it.

"So the church matters," you say. "All right, but I'm not sure I'm ready for all the doctrines and teachings that the church believes. Prayer, for example . . . I don't know how it works, what it means, or whether I want to start dong it. It's sort of spooky, if you ask me."

Read on, if you dare.

Chapter Nine

"Is Prayer for Real?"

Luke 11:1–13

In *The Adventures of Huckleberry Finn,* Huck gives his views on the subject of prayer. He says:

> Miss Watson, she took me in the closet and prayed, but nothing come of it. She told me to pray every day and whatever I asked for I would get it. But it warn't so. I tried it. Once I got a fish line, but no hooks. It warn't any good to me without hooks. I tried for the hooks three or four times, but somehow I couldn't make it work. By and by, I asked Miss Watson to try for me, but she said I was a fool. She never told me why, and I couldn't make it out noway.
>
> I set down one time back in the woods and had a long think about it. I says to myself if a body can get anything they pray for, why don't Deacon Winn get back the money he lost on pork? And why can't the widow get back her silver snuff box that was stole? Why can't Miss Watson fat up? No, says I to myself, there ain't nothin' in it.[1]

A lot of other people in today's secular marketplace have decided "there ain't nothin' in it." To many of them, prayer has been tried and found lacking, and since it doesn't work, doesn't provide any vital resource out of which to live, it's unnecessary . . . a waste of time . . . boring.

Candor requires me to confess that there's also considerable uncertainty among us Christian believers concerning prayer. It's not outsiders alone who raise the question, "Is prayer for real?"

My own experiences with prayer and with people tell me that some of the trouble lies in our confusion about what prayer is and does. Some people see it as magic words. Just use the right words, punch the right buttons, and God will come through. German preacher and writer Helmut Thieleke reports on a national survey in which eighty-six percent of the people said they sometimes prayed, but only sixty-eight percent of them acknowledged that they really believed in God! Even when they're unsure about God, people are willing to try the "formula" of prayer. As Huck Finn discovered, however, prayer as right words, magic formulas, or correct incantation doesn't work. It's a view on prayer that many of us have (or should have) outgrown.

Others have used prayer as a sort of "hot line" to God, to be used only in emergency situations. In Shakespeare's *The Tempest*, the mariners in a storm resort to this understanding of prayer with their cries, "All is lost! To prayers, to prayers!" Praying during the tight spots of life is surely legitimate, but it won't work as a steady diet. One problem is that it attempts to manipulate God into operating on our schedule and agenda . . . which he obviously doesn't do.

Some folks are disillusioned with prayer because it aggravates the tension between the heart and the head. In the 1985 movie, *Trip to Bountiful*, Geraldine Page won an Oscar for her performance as Carrie Watts. Carrie is a woman who wants to make a return visit to Bountiful, a Texas community that doesn't exist anymore. Sitting in the bus station, she tells a young woman about the big adventure she's had, slipping away from her children, getting a bus ticket, and now being very close to her long anticipated dream. "I guess the Lord's just with me today," says Carrie. She continues:

> Wonder why the Lord's not with us every day. Sure would be nice if he was. M-m-m-m, well, maybe then we wouldn't appreciate it so much on those days when he is with us. Or maybe he's with us always, and we just don't know it.

I think Carrie spoke for many who suspect that God drops in and out of life on a mysterious whim. That's pretty unsettling, intellectually.

You see, there are times when we feel strongly the need for outside help—for divine intervention—and so we ask in prayer for a sufficiency beyond our own. The problem comes, however, not from the heart, but from the head. God made life to operate along dependable, predictable lines—the laws of gravity, of aging and perishability, of interdependence with one another in accidents or crimes. For good or ill, that's life, and God seems committed to letting life operate on that game plan (cf. above, Chapter Three). Prayer feels like trying to persuade God to go back on that plan whenever it damages us and those we love. So that the conflict of emotion versus intellect seems worsened and intensified by the act of prayer.

The language of prayer often puts people off. For some of us church types, prayer seems to be a blending of certain beautiful sounds that we present to God, sort of a verbal "gift" to the deity. The problem is that such "adorned" praying can create distance from our actual needs and from God. There's nothing wrong with Victorian English; it just isn't the language we use anymore. My own early recollections of prayer in church and home are of those adorned sounds. "You" became "thou"; "were" became "wert"; "was" got changed into "wast"; "has" into "hast"; "your" became "thy"; and "your" was "thine." It all sounded exalted and serious and reverent . . . and distant. In recent years, the reaction to this on the part of certain evangelicals and charismatics has turned prayer into a "love ya' Jesus" pep rally. Here God becomes such a "divine buddy" that all sense of awe and mystery are lost.

Of course, some people have given up on prayer just because they're tired of trying. More than anything, this objection is probably tied to expectations. Bruce Larson says somewhere that a lot of folks bring to prayer the same mindset that a gambler brings to a slot machine: "It won't cost much, and I might hit the jackpot." When they don't hit it (whatever that may mean for them), they just move on, deciding that prayer is a waste of time and not for them.

Yet, all the while, despite these objections from the marketplace (and from immature but honest Christians as well), prayer remains an important ingredient in the spiritual stew which is served up by the church. How realistic is that? What good can prayer possibly do? How can we defend it as something meaningful for the nineties?

My own understanding of prayer grows out of one simple and basic fact, namely, that Christian living begins and grows in a personal relationship with God. Everything that touches my life touches that partnership. All the joys and pains of my daily pilgrimage are set within that awareness. Now, nothing much about

Christian faith, including prayer, seems very logical from the outside, looking in. It may seem irrational or curious or downright silly to the detached observer. But within the framework of faith, there is a blessed good sense about it all.

It's a little like looking at a family from the outside. If you were to stare through the window at a Thanksgiving meal or at a family gathered for Christmas Eve, you might conclude that the customs and traditions of that particular family appear trite or stupid. Even the words they use with each other, the terms of endearment or humor with which they address each other, may seem sticky and sentimental from the outside. But if you belong to that family, those words make warm and perfect sense because they are the words and phrases and customs and traditions of a close relationship.

So if prayer be words flung against an alien sky, it is boring and useless and unrealistic. But if prayer be the language of love and trust inside faith's framework, it becomes a logical necessity. If God loves and befriends us, then prayer is one of the most natural things in life for the Christian believer.

> No tongue or pen can show
> The love of Jesus, what it is.
> None but his loved ones know.

To understand prayer, then, I have to start with the salvation of God extended to me in Jesus Christ.

Growing out of that rootage, I experience prayer as three or four things. First of all, as *communication*—simply because any relationship is built on communication. As obvious as such a statement may seem, this simple fact has clarified my concept of prayer on more than one occasion. You see, a lot of my struggle with prayer has revolved around two questions, namely, "If God knows everything, why pray?" and "If prayer is not an attempt to coerce God, why bother?" My discovery has been that such questions miss the whole point of prayer. Overwhelmingly, Jesus' teaching on prayer indicates that it is one facet of a human-divine dialogue that builds a companionship of trust and openness. This means that I bring to my relationship with God the concerns that I bring to any other significant relationship. "Prayer," wrote William Barclay, "is simply taking life to God."

This dialogue will certainly include an occasional cry for help. According to Jesus, God is the kind of Father who cares about the deep and daily needs of our lives. In the eleventh chapter of Luke, one of the longest texts we have on Jesus and his understanding of prayer, our Lord tells about a friend who awakens his neighbor and asks for bread to set before a stranger. Palestinian hospitality required such treatment of one who, traveling at night, needed a place to stay. The neighbor at first refuses to help, contending that he will disturb his family (in the typical Palestinian home, they would likely be sleeping in the same room). The friend is persistent, however, and Jesus' point in this story seems to be to encourage us to "go on asking, go on seeking, go on knocking." (The Greek verbs in this instance are present imperatives, indicating continuous action.) Why should we keep asking, seeking, and knocking? Because God, like a good friend, is approachable and is sensitive to our needs.

In this same text, Jesus describes God as being not a calloused, cruel father, but one who will lovingly and honestly respond to the needs of his children. God, says Jesus, "will give the Holy Spirit to those who ask him" (vs. 13). That's important, for it means that in the deepening relationship that I have with God, I can be sure that he will provide me with himself and with all of the resources that that presence can bring. And that, by the way, is about as meaningful a resource as any relationship can provide!

My relationship with God also means the sharing of my failures. It isn't that God needs a briefing from me; he knows about my sins and shortcomings. But any genuine relationship calls for mutual honesty and vulnerability. You know how that works in a friendship. If you and I are good friends and you see me write a check and sign your name to it, that's going to impact our relationship until I talk with you about it. The same is true in a marriage. If a spouse sins against the relationship by adulterous behavior, though you may both know it, the relationship is in jeopardy until the facts are owned and dealt with by both parties.

Now God has become vulnerable to me. He has opened up to me as fully as possible in Jesus of Nazareth. He has become subject to the human situation, vulnerable to the weakness of the cross. Confession and openness on my part helps match up with his investment in our relationship. So prayer is a way of being open with God about the failures which both of us know about already.

For me, then, prayer is a means of relating to God. It's the language needed for the communication which sustains our partnership. As my partnership with God becomes more personal and more open, I am able to draw on the strength that that provides. Consequently, as I grow older, I find myself rarely asking God for *things* when I pray; I usually ask him to provide those inner, deeper resources that our companionship makes possible.

A second thing: prayer as *pilgrimage*. In Jesus' model prayer, he refers to things like food, failures, and interpersonal conflicts. So we are encouraged to pray about the daily grind. In 1 Thessalonians, Paul says to pray constantly, or "without ceasing" (5:17). What does that mean? That prayer cannot be restricted to a routine at bedtime, mealtime, or worship time. That it is not limited to a particular posture or a particular set of words. If prayer is the language of relationship with God, then it ought to be synonymous with all of life, for my relationship with God touches all of my life. I really like the prayer of a child who was asked to say grace at a meal:

> Thank you, Lord, for this meal,
> We know you are the giver.
> But thank you, Lord, most of all
> That we ain't having liver.

Anything that matters to us matters to God . . . liver included!

This means that one does not have to withdraw from the world to encounter God. He is present in the push and passion of daily pilgrimage. Every relationship, business deal, decision, and intention . . . it's all spiritual. So when we try to isolate prayer from life's real concerns, it becomes sterile.

I love the sentiment, if not the theology, of a prayer that I read some years ago in the *Baptist Peacemaker*. It is attributed to Captain Jack Hayes during the Mexican War at the battle of Palo Alto:

> Oh, Lord, we are about to join battle with vastly superior numbers of the enemy, and Heavenly Father, we would mighty like for you to be on our side and help us. But if you can't do it, for Christ's sake, don't go over to the Mexicans. Just lie low and keep in the dark and you will see one of the dangdest fights you've ever seen.

Discounting the civil religion and the racism of such a prayer, you can't fault it for lack of honesty!

Our feelings and fears, our anger and anxiety, our happiness and hope . . . all are the legitimate stuff of real praying, because all are the legitimate stuff of personal pilgrimage. It's on that daily journey that we experience some of the most important moments of our relationship with God. Paul is "on the go" when he unexpectedly encounters Christ on the Damascus road. God confronts Jacob during the heat of his escape from Esau. Of course, for the twelve men who followed after Jesus, the presence of God was more obvious in the way he lived daily than in any other . . . and he lived a controversial life in a turbulent world.

Since God is at work in the world in many different ways, to "pray constantly" surely means to maintain awareness of his presence, his caring, and his reaching out to the concrete needs of persons. When I join hands with him in such a ministry, I commune most meaningfully with him. It's no accident that our word "liturgy" means literally "the work of the people." Work gets done in sanctuaries of worship, all right, but it gets done mostly in the marketplace of daily activities. Therefore, God cannot be given his "due" at stated times only. His due—and the focus of valid praying—is our involvement with him in the ongoing journey of struggle and ministry and healing. So prayer is not an isolated act. It is that mindset of faith which expects God's guidance in all of living.

Next, then, there is prayer as *reinforcement*. The text in Luke 11 says that the disciples found Jesus "praying at a certain place, and when he ceased, one of his disciples said to him, 'Lord, teach us to pray . . . '" (vs. 1). That's a strange request from people who probably learned to pray at their mothers' knees and in the synagogue services. If they were conscientious Jews, they might already be praying at least three times every day! Yet they must have thought that they could learn something unusual about prayer from Jesus. It think it's instructive that the occasion that drew out of them this request was a time of specific withdrawal for Jesus. If anyone ever knew the presence of God in the continuum of life, Jesus certainly did. No one ever lived in the daily grind with more of an awareness of God's nearness. Yet, Jesus did not disdain the practice of periodic withdrawal for evaluation, reflection, quietness, and the fine-tuning of a Father-Son relationship.

When someone asked Eric Fromm for a down-to-earth solution to the problems of modern life, he responded, "The experience of stillness. You have to stop in order to change direction." I think Jesus knew that, and so he had times of stillness and aloneness. We know it, too, many of us, but we tend to plunge ahead with increased activity, then wonder why our lives are so shallow and fragmented. Like everything else in his life, Jesus' example of prayer challenges us to follow. Unless we do, we will miss the reinforcement, the centering, and the clarifying that is so crucial to effective discipleship.

Thus, the routine of prayer at a definite time and place is certainly valid as long as it does not become an escape or a dull habit. As was true in the practice of Jesus, I have found that the encountering of God in all of life often sends me back to specific times of prayer. It's true that my prayer may mostly take the form of ministry in the world, but I desperately need periods of solitude with him during which I can focus my feelings and thoughts and needs. Unless I do that, I will likely miss his presence and direction amidst the sound and fury of everyday life. All of life ought to be prayer, but that's totally unrealistic without those times when we have silence and aloneness before God.

My wife's twenty-year battle with rheumatoid arthritis has taught both of us enormous lessons about many things, including faith and patience. In recent years, she has begun to find great strength in spiritual meditation. Much of her exuberance for life, her sensitivity to persons, and her deep sense of God's presence grow out of those periodic times of stillness and relaxation, during which she is genuinely refreshed.

So much of the power of prayer seems to lie in the discipline of praying. Your method or structure or schedule may differ from my wife's or mine or somebody else's. In fact, it should be very personal because meaningful friendships are not based on rules concocted up by others. But there *should be* schedule and structure and method in your prayer life. Otherwise, it becomes hit-and-miss, and that's pretty weak.

In some of the most strategic moments of his life, we find Jesus at prayer. It was certainly much more than a tradition that had been passed down to him. He had a tough job bringing to people, not what they wanted or expected, but what they needed. The temptation to be and to give only what they expected was most difficult. The only thing able to sustain him was his relationship with the Father, and prayer was a way of reinforcing that relationship—of keeping the center of his life truly internal. That need for centering is ours, as well. In the thick of the swirling, shifting winds of public opinion and peer pressure, prayer as periodic reinforcement nurtures a meaningful relationship with God.

One other thing, prayer as *possibility*. In the longer version of the model prayer (Matt 6), there is the request "thy kingdom come, thy will be done on earth as it is in Heaven." That simple petition, it seems to me, makes prayer rationally defensible. It says that God is active in both earthly and heavenly dimensions. He created the world but is not imprisoned within it or limited by it. God operates on our level of reality, but he operates on a higher level, as well.

What we call "miracle" therefore, may in fact be God's normal activity. As inexplicable as it may be to our logic, it may be perfectly natural to him. *Our* prior theological assumptions may not be altogether consistent with God's way of behaving.

Let me suggest a feeble analogy here. I learned about gravity in a grade school science class, and I knew immediately that I'd latched on to something that would be enduring. Soon, however, I learned that there are other worlds and even universes where the law of gravity is not operative. I also learned arithmetic as a child, and I felt secure in knowing that the basic fact of life will always be two plus two equals four and three plus three equals six, etc. Now, my friends who are into advanced algebra tell me that there's a world where such arithmetic facts don't operate anymore. When I began to study poetry, I learned that one of the things that marks poetry is its rhyme. That held true until I discovered free verse, and the reality of rhyme just didn't operate anymore.

I hope you see my point.

God is not captive to all our earthly foregone conclusions. Therefore, living in partnership with God keeps open a lot of possibilities . . . and it's all right to ask for his help. That keeps life open-ended and our pilgrimage exciting.

French biologist Alexis Carrel reminded us of the vast possibilities. When we pray, he said, we link ourselves with "the inexhaustible motive power that spins the universe." Quaker scholar Richard Foster *personalized* this truth without reducing it. In *Celebration of Discipline*, he wrote, "If we genuinely love people, we desire for them far more than it is within our power to give, and that will cause us to pray."

Prayer is a tremendous possibility! Who knows what the Lord of heaven and earth, who is also a loving Father, might want to do in our lives?

Is prayer for real, then? I think it is, because of the example of Jesus and the sturdiness of life that I see in those Christians who do it. Along the Texas Gulf Coast where we live, we know about hurricanes and heavy thunderstorms. Often, after the heavy winds have passed, we see giant trees uprooted and destroyed, which before the storm had looked impregnable to any assault imaginable. I'm neither botanist nor tree surgeon, but I wonder if some of those trees were top-heavy. Too much of trunk and branch and not enough of deep roots. I am a pastor, and I see an awful lot of lives broken down for that very reason. Outwardly strong and successful, they are without deep, spiritual roots, and when the storms of life come, as they do to us all, a life without such roots can be easily toppled.

In the marketplace of the nineties, the need for God is real . . . as is the need for faith . . . and for prayer. I suspect that the biggest problem most of us have with praying is not theological but practical . . . we just don't do it. Maybe it's time to change that.

"*Is Prayer for Real?*" 113

What, then, of death and beyond? The yearning for faith grows strong when we face that subject. But is belief a cop-out here? Aren't we really dealing with wishful thinking?

Maybe . . . but maybe not.

Chapter Ten

"What Happens When We Die?"

1 John 3:1–3

In the uniqueness that is our humanness, we live with or without meaning and direction . . . and in these pages, I have contended that choosing to live with or without God has an awful lot to say about that. It is that basic premise of our focus on this journey through some of life's enduring questions.

Now, when you come right down to it, there are only two life or death issues: life and death. And you deal with both of them on the basis of faith or unfaith. When the subject of death and beyond is broached, there are some modern persons, steeped in the secularization of the times, who immediately put up their barriers. "Don't talk to me about that old pie-in-the-sky stuff. I'm struggling to handle this world; I don't have time to worry about that." So faith is quickly dismissed as irrelevant, and the struggle to believe ends abruptly . . . or so it seems.

I want to say two things in response to such an attitude. First, we *do* bother with death. In fact, we are much bothered with it. No matter that our vaccines, our antibiotics, our polyunsaturates, our oat bran, and our aerobics keep death at bay much longer than before. No matter that our commitment to pleasure and the full scheduling of leisure time keep us pushing away any thoughts about death. No matter that our preoccupation with youthful looks and lifestyle keeps us denying the process of aging and dying. The truth is that we modern people are troubled by death. Why else should we go to such lengths of avoidance and denial?

Second, in response to the reality of death, we can live with despair or with hope. Many people default into despair as they consider the prospect of death. Helmut Thielicke recalls psychiatrist Alfred Hocke's discussion of "life's law of perishability." Hocke writes that though we human beings see this law at work all around us in animals and plants, we just cannot resign ourselves to our own perishability. Man "carries within himself an intensely subjective world," he says. He also says that "it seems unbearable to him that this world is simply to be wiped out. It is unbearable simply to collapse beside the road while the others continue, chattering as though nothing had happened. He concludes, "The power of this feeling defies logic."[1]

He's right. That is a powerful feeling. Our own perishability, then . . . nothing. Given such a perspective, we will eventually end in despair.

But that's not the only option. We can choose hope as we ponder death and the beyond. This is where the message of Jesus Christ is again "good news" for the people of the nineties.

For nearly twenty centuries now, the followers of Jesus Christ have espoused life after death as a consequence of faith in God. We've seldom agreed on the exact form and substance, but we've based our hope on the teaching and the life of Jesus—especially on his resurrection—and on the faith and logic of some of his earliest followers like Paul, John, and others.

"Heaven" quickly became the church's way of talking about this hope. Some of us feel that heaven is a place, a definite locality beyond time and space. Others—believing that death takes us into a sphere beyond the time/space continuum—see heaven as a state of awareness. They would not posit existence in any disembodied form, but still they do not see us dwelling in a heavenly locality in the same way that we are now writing or reading these words and sitting in a particular locality. So, "state of awareness" is their way of describing a heaven that is beyond this life. Still others are committed to the concept of heaven as continuing existence for all believers, but they maintain a reverent agnosticism concerning its exact location or the details of its environment.

Moving from faith to logic, we quickly discover that there's no universal agreement on how to answer the question about life after death. The latest Gallup poll I've seen indicates that more than seventy percent of Americans believe in life after death, but this is not an issue that can be resolved by "majority opinion." Besides, those who oppose the belief in any future existence mount some pretty strong arguments. For one thing, it is unprovable, they insist. We don't have any witnesses who have returned from the grave to tell us about it, and the resurrection of Jesus would be classified with all other ancient myths concerning resurrected gods. Furthermore, psychic research is as yet inconclusive. There seem to be as many charlatans in the field as there are serious researchers, and though this area of psychic phenomena may yield rich dividends, as of now, its findings cannot be cited as conclusive evidence for life beyond the grave.

Others insist that life after death would be unethical. To so believe would devalue life in the present; it would easily minimize our concern with the here and now struggles of life.

Still others insist that life after death is impossible. Bertrand Russell once said that he could not see how any fire, any heroism, or any force in all the universe could possibly sustain a human life beyond the grave. Since our bodies do not survive death, our consciousness cannot. Our senses are dependent upon our physical organisms; so when those organisms die, we die. That's all there is to that.

But those who seek to use logic in their argument *for* life after death say, for instance, that the purposefulness of the universe somehow demands it. However we view the natural order, there does seem to be design within it. If, therefore, this universe did not have its origin in the purely chaotic or the purely accidental, the life of humankind calls for ultimate meaning. Now, since we are robbed of so much of that meaning by the inequities and the imperfections of life, there must be a balancing of accounts somehow, somewhere. The fact that there are so many who never really have a chance for meaningful life—physically, mentally, or psychologically—calls for another chance and a straightening out of affairs. So these lives of ours demand a longer term of existence than life on this planet alone affords.

The value of human life itself is also used as a argument for life after death. The scientists tell us that this planet will die someday (unless we kill it first!). They've predicted that the earth will become a cold dark sphere unable to support human life in a few million years. When that happens, so goes the argument, unless there is some ultimacy to human existence that extends beyond this planetary existence, the human story will be finished. To view man/woman in terms of this world only therefore, conserves nothing, wastes everything, and means that it's all a silly joke . . . a senseless, useless existence.

But let's take another look at *faith* as a way of answering our question about life after death. I certainly don't believe that Christian faith sets logic aside, but I know that there are many points of conviction in the Christian life where faith has to take precedence over the purely logical and observable. This whole area of human survival is one of those conviction points.

The biblical perspective on death is permeated with a refreshing honesty. The Bible is not a death-denying book. Men and women are viewed as "grass" and "dust" in their temporariness. The Bible nowhere insults our intelligence by playing down death and its attendant grief. In fact, the scriptures refer pretty consistently to death as "the enemy."

It follows, then, that faith in God is no total anesthetic for the pain that tears at us when we, or someone we love, confront dying. Such pain is part of our humanity, given us by a Creator who knew that creatures capable of love and involvement with each other must also be capable of being hurt by separation and death. Joy and pain are inevitable threads in the fabric of caring, and Christians are *not* into denying that. We believers in Christ are not called to be somehow more-than-human in our times of loss. In the wake of life's tragedy and sorrow, it is a sick faith that takes our hope in the risen Christ and twists it into a rationale for false fronts and pious denials. Paul writes to the Thessalonians that we should not "grieve as others do who have no hope," and I certainly agree . . . but we *should* grieve!

We die, say some of the biblical writers, because of our sin. "For as in Adam all die, so also in Christ shall all be made alive" (1 Cor 15:22). "The wages of sin is death" (Rom 6:23). In instances like these, it's almost impossible to know whether "death" refers to physical death or to a "second death" that is synonymous with separation from God after physical death. In other places, the writers of the Bible accept death as a fact of our humanity. We are part of a created order that is mortal, and story after story in the

Bible ends with the fact of physical death without any particular spiritual significance attached. The biblical view is clearly that there is an inevitability about our mortality.

What, then, about life after death?

Remember, please, that the biblical writers were not systematic theologians. Their views on this subject are quite varied. Despite that, in both Old and New Testament thought, something of human essence survives physical death.

In the Old Testament, it's a dim shadowy existence beyond the grave . . . Sheol is the term for the "netherworld" to which the dead go. And with but a handful of exceptions, we don't find a full and meaningful existence beyond the grave in the minds of the Hebrew writers.

The Greek world, on the other hand, had a strong belief in life after death couched in its view of personal immortality or "the immortality of the soul." The Greek view was that when the body died, the "soul" was released to its preexistent state. I'm sure that the Greek view of immortality increasingly influenced theology as Christianity moved away from its Jewish moorings and into the larger world. Furthermore, it's quite likely that some of the New Testament writers were influenced by this "immortality" concept. The dominant New Testament idea, however, is that of resurrection—resurrection of the body. The Hebrews simply did not conceive of man as soul without body. To them, a human being was a totality. If he/she survives death, it will not be as a disembodied spirit; it will be as a resurrected body (though not altogether the physical body).

Actually, the Hebrew view takes death more seriously than the Greek one. When we die, we die . . . but we live in anticipation of resurrection. This idea of the resurrection of the dead was becoming pretty strong in Hebrew thought by New Testament times. It was based largely on the expected vindication by God of his people, and the righteous dead were to share in that time of vindication. Paradise (a Persian word) was thought to be the abode of the righteous dead. So when Jesus used this word on the cross to give hope to a dying thief (hardly one of the "righteous dead"!), he was going against the grain of popular belief (cf. Luke 23:32–43). Later Christian thinkers used the term paradise less and began to speak instead of heaven. It is that term, of course, that remains in wide use among us.

Another part of Sheol was *gehenna*, the place of the wicked dead. Associated with the Valley of Hinnom just outside Jerusalem, it was a place of pagan worship that in Jesus' day had become a rubbish heap. So some of the images of gehenna are obvious references to the characteristics of this valley dump ("where their worm does not die and the fire is not quenched"—Mark 9:48). Later Christian writers came to use "hell" as their characteristic term, and so it remains today.

When Jesus talked about life after death, he did it pretty directly. I count nine times that he referred to gehenna or hell, and his words on the subject followed the rabbinic teachings of his time, namely, sin is serious, and the life dominated by it is separated from God now and in the hereafter. So Jesus didn't talk about hell or judgment to scare people; he did it to say that life and the way we live it matters. It's a precious gift that we can use for good or ill, and we *will* be held accountable for our use of it. When you study his sayings on hell, that's what comes through. And, interestingly, those sayings about hell reveal a concern with our *actual deeds* more than with our theology or our church membership.

A senior deacon in our church told me a great story that his preacher father had told years ago about a rich man who met Saint Peter as he tried to enter Heaven. He was told by Peter that he could not enter because he'd made lots of money and had never shared it with anyone. "You're right," he admitted. Then he brightened a bit and said, "But I once gave a poor hungry soul two dollars. Take that information to God and see what it will get me." Peter walked away, but very quickly returned with this information: "I've been instructed to tell you to take your two dollars . . . and go to hell!"

I don't know if not giving money will keep anybody out of heaven, but I do know that Jesus said we're accountable for helping the hungry, the thirsty, the stranger, the prisoner, the needy, and that our response to such need is our response to him (cf. Matt 25:31ff).

Jesus was severe in his warnings about hell. We don't need to try to soften that . . . we just need to hear it and take it seriously. It says that we're responsible for our lives and the choices we make, and that our accountability involves eternal consequences. I like the way C. S. Lewis put it in *The Great Divorce*. He said that in the end there are only two kinds of people, "those who say to God, 'Thy will be done,' and those to whom God says in the end,'*thy* will be done.'" Hell, someone said, may be the final tribute that God pays to the dignity of the human being. We *are* accountable.

Now, when Jesus talked about heaven, it was usually as the place where God resides. In his clearest references to life after death, he doesn't use the term at all, but his meaning is obvious. "I am the resurrection and the life. He who believes in me, though he die, yet shall he live. And whoever lives and believes in me shall never die . . . " (John 11:25–26). "And when I go and prepare a place for you, I will come again and take you to myself, that where I am you may be also" (John 14:3).

Taking their cue from sayings like these, Christian thinkers naturally came to conceive of heaven as the place where we are with Christ. The biblical writers neither speak with a singular voice, nor do they give cut-and-dried answers. In fact, they often leave us at loose ends. One of the reasons we don't have a more carefully worked out answer to the question of life after death is that the early Christians expected Christ's return almost immediately. Since only a minority of believers would have to be raised from the dead, their focus is on that anticipated return . . . not on twenty centuries or more of waiting for the resurrection of believers.

As Christian thinkers began to expand the concept of heaven and hell, they did (in some cases) some unbelievably bad things to them. They majored on literalizing the New Testament imagery—torture and fire in hell and golden streets in heaven, for example. Unfortunately, it is this kind of emphasis rather than Jesus' seriousness about our accountability that has carried over even into modern times. In defense of the New Testament preachers and teachers themselves, a quick reminder, please, that the earliest Christian preaching in the book of Acts contains only scant and indirect references to heaven and hell. In fact, the only mention of hell or hades is in a reference to the death of Christ in Acts 2:31. Apparently, this emphasis did not become a part of "gospel preaching" until late in and beyond the New Testament era.

So, cutting through all the scripture and the tradition and the history, what *is* the basis of our hope of life after death? If we choose to live by faith in the risen Christ, what awaits us?

There are three brief verses in the epistle of First John that form the basis for my answers to those questions—answers that are affirmations of personal faith. The first is this: *God's love is more powerful than death.*

> See what love the Father has given us that we should be called children of God, and so we are. (1 John 3:1)

My view of life after death is solidly based, not on speculation or logic about human immortality, but on an event—the resurrection of Jesus Christ. Early Christian believers looked at that event and concluded, "Here is the greatest victory of love over hate, of good over evil, of life over death in human history!" Their conviction was that we become children of God through personal faith in the risen Christ, and when we make a faith commitment to him as Lord, we tap into the most powerful force in all the world—God's love. If death did not finally defeat such a love on that Roman cross where Jesus died, we who live in relationship with him will not be defeated by death either.

William Cullen Bryant watched a wild bird flying and disappearing into the fading sunset, and he wrote

> Thou'rt gone, the abyss of heaven
> Hath swallowed up thy form; yet, on my heart
> Deeply hath sunk the lesson thou hast given,
> And shall not soon depart.

And here is that lesson:

> He who, from zone to zone,
> Guides through the boundless sky thy certain flight,

In the long way that I must tread alone
Will lead my steps aright.²

Choosing to base your life on Jesus Christ means that you can trust God's love for the future.

When Catholic theologian Hans Küng was asked to give one of the addresses at the memorial service for Karl Barth, he recalled a conversation he'd had with Barth in which the subject of life after death arose. Barth said,

> And when the day comes when I have to appear before my Lord, then I will not come with my deeds, with the volumes of my Dogmatics in the basket upon my back. . . . I also shall not say I have always meant well, I had good faith. No, at that time, I shall say only one thing—Lord, be merciful to me, a poor sinner.³

Heaven is ours because of a love that forgives and accepts us, and that kind of love is more powerful than death. Christ did not demolish death; he *did* conquer it. His promise to all who will follow him in faith is, "Because I live you shall live also."

I don't know and I don't worry about the population of heaven. I believe in hell because I believe in human accountability. But I'm a reverent agnostic about the roll call of hell or heaven simply because that roll call is God's prerogative, not mine. With all my mind and heart, however, I believe that faith in Jesus Christ leads to heaven and a life beyond, not as the reward for "being good," but just because that's where the road of companionship leads. Because, with HelmutThieleke, "I am already the comrade of him whose faithfulness to me will never end."

So my faith is rooted in that historical Christ event that broke the grip of death's awesome power . . . Christ raised from the dead, the first fruits of those who sleep. "What love the Father has given us." Indeed!

My second answer/affirmation is that *our growth will be enhanced, not stopped, by death*. The writer of First John says this:

> Beloved, we are God's children now. It does not yet appear what we shall be, but we know that when he appears we shall be like him, for we shall see him as he is. (vs. 2)

"We are God's children *now*." We've already begun a pilgrimage toward wholeness and real (eternal) life. We won't make it to full maturity in this time-and-space dimension of earthly living. There will be work to do on the other side. Though death may change the dimension of our growth, it will not change our direction—the process of becoming like Christ. The important thing about heaven, then, is not its exact location (it's obviously beyond our time-and-space awareness), but that it is that realm where we will know the continuation and the expansion of a journey that has already begun. "It does not yet appear what we shall be."

Like the New Testament writers, we must struggle to describe heaven in terms of poetry and parable and analogy. It will certainly be well beyond anything we can even imagine. But it *will* be home. The Lord whom we know and love and serve will cross over with us to make it a hospitable place.

A sense of unfulfillment really does dog our steps in this life, and I believe that heaven will bring us nearer our potential as God's children than ever. In the third chapter of Ecclesiastes, the writer makes the striking statement that God "has put eternity into man's mind." That suggests, at least, that we humans hunger, not for an extension of known existence, but for a new dimension of that existence. When we come down to the end of our lives, there are still blank pages in us waiting to be filled. The God who gave us minds to ask the enduring questions of life will surely some day give us answers.

Victor Hugo worked for nearly fifty years writing prose, poetry, history, philosophy, and drama. Near the end of a busy and productive life, he said, "I appear to myself not to have said a thousandth part of what is within me; and when I am laid in the tomb, I shall not reckon that my life is finished."[4] Likewise, it is my conviction that no Christian pilgrim has exhausted his/her possibilities at death.

So what form of existence may we expect in the life beyond? Paul, in writing to the Corinthians, says, "This perishable nature must put on the imperishable, and this mortal nature must put on immortality." Good Hebrew that he was, Paul could not conceive of immortality as continued existence in some disembodied form. He obviously has some sort of resurrected "body" in mind. So, in

Philippians, he says, we await "the Lord Jesus Christ who will transform the body of your humble state into conformity with the body of his glory . . . ." The writer of First John says clearly that "we shall be like him because we shall see him just as he is."

Does that mean that our forms will be recognizable? There's no clear-cut and unanimous answer. Jesus did appear after the resurrection in recognizable form. They knew him as the one with whom they'd shared those pre-crucifixion years. So, it may well be that while the post-death form may be different from our physical form, the identity will remain. That's not too far-fetched when you consider that, except for the nerve cells, every cell of your body changes every seven or eight years . . . yet your identity remains. So a biological change occurring in physical death need not rob you of your unique and essential identity.

While he was pastor at New York's Riverside Church, William Sloane Coffin told of visiting with a woman whose future funeral service he had been asked to conduct. In her late seventies and physically ravaged by cancer of the liver, she and Coffin engaged in a frank discussion on death and life beyond. When the pastor got up to leave, she kissed him tenderly, and he said to her, "Maybe we'll meet again." She smiled and said, "Not as I am." To which the pastor could only reply, "Then not as I am either." Based on what we know of biology, that would seem an impossibility. But, given God's power operating in a fresh dimension of reality, I believe that Paul's "spiritual body" will be part of that reality. Wordsworth reminds us that we now live with:

> Hope that can never die
> Effort and expectation and desire
> And something evermore about to be.

Someday, hope and possibility will be realized!

One final affirmation about Christian faith and the fact of death. *We can live with clear direction now.* Verse 3 of our First John text says, "And everyone who thus hopes in him purifies himself as he is pure." Christian hope can give purity, clarity, focus for daily living . . . that's what our writer says. If we can rest assured that we're sustained by God's love, we can get on with the important tasks to be done in the here and now.

So, I reject the notion that the Christian hope of life after death somehow makes earthly life less precious. I reject the proposition also that faith is an opiate or an escapism from dealing with the issues and the struggles of this life. The fact that I choose to live by faith in Jesus Christ, and that that settles the issue of what to expect when I die, frees me to live most responsibly in the here and now. An ultimate question has been answered . . . now I may work and risk and serve! It's precisely because "our commonwealth is in heaven" that we may be full citizens of *this* world. There's nothing like a long-range goal to keep present perspectives clear. And since the sting of death has been drawn by Christ, I am truly free to live now . . . seriously, fully, openly. Hope, said Thomas Merton, frees our hands so that we can work with them!

Several years ago, I read about a college professor who conducted an interesting experiment in one of his classes. He passed an imaginary sentence of death on his students and gave them six months to live. They were to go to a mortuary and make arrangements for their funerals, and they were to write out their own obituaries. He wanted to find out how they felt about facing the ancient enemy. At the end of the experiment, he reported that the overwhelming impression was that these students were wasting their lives.

As I read that story, I remembered that Elizabeth Kübler-Ross, the noted researcher with the terminally ill, had reached much the same conclusion. She said that the greatest lesson that she and her colleagues had learned from their patients was, "LIVE . . . so you do not have to look back and say, 'Oh, how I have wasted my life.'"[5]

Life is scarce because of death, more precious because of death. So the message of Christian faith about heaven is not escapism.

On the contrary, faith is the dynamic that frees us from argument and anxiety about the ultimate time tables and road maps. It frees us, instead, to be deeply and redemptively involved in *today*.

James Stewart of Edinburgh told of a wartime nightduring World War I when troops going out to the front the next day had gathered in a large hall for an evening's entertainment. When it was over, a young officer stood to thank the entertainers for the enjoyable evening. He thanked them in a humorous and genial way, and then suddenly his countenance changed. He spoke now in a totally different tone, "We're crossing to the trenches of France tomorrow, very possibly to our deaths. Is there anybody here who can tell us how to die?" There followed an awkward, silent moment when no one knew what to say. Then one of the young women who had performed earlier made her way to the stage and began to sing the great aria from *Elijah*, "O Rest in the Lord." Of course, there were few dry eyes when she finished.

Can anybody tell us how to die? Jesus, crucified and buried, can tell us.

Can anybody tell us how to live? Jesus, risen from the dead, can tell us.

Such is the faith of the New Testament about death and beyond. It's my faith, too. The God who now loves and sustains us now will *not* desert us at the end.

Epilogue

Only time, or eternity perhaps, will tell how many of the foregoing answers are true and lasting. For now . . . for me . . . for many who share my faith community . . . they are sound.

Still, the questions abide. In fact, some of them grow in intensity as I grow older. I'm more puzzled by suffering, more troubled by the power of evil and the evil of power, more curious about the ways of God, more interested in the mystery of life beyond the grave, and more certain of my/our insatiable thirst for hope.

So, Christian faith abides . . . mostly, I believe, because it *must*. Last year on a March afternoon, about twenty of us sat at the Institute of Religion in the Texas Medical Center for a lengthy dialogue with Roman Catholic scholar Hans Küng. The religious world was awash with threats on the life of Salman Rushdie, with televangelism scandals, and with a statistical spiral that continued downward in the mainline churches. My question to Professor Küng was something like, "In light of all the craziness that happens in the name of religion, why does *anybody* who's a rational citizen of this modern world still buy into it?" His answer came quickly. "Because it's there," he said. "Because the materialism and the other alternatives since World War II have not worked . . . and the hunger for faith remains."

Of course! A self-serving hedonism leaves us empty of purpose. A rampant materialism comes up shallow. Even an optimistic humanism increasingly disappoints us. In the most secularized society this world has yet known, the hunger obviously remains. So I think maybe there's a place for books like this one . . . for the affirmation of a faith that grows . . . and for an ongoing spiritual quest.

I hope you agree.

Amen, . . . and welcome to the journey.

Notes

Introduction

[1] *A Circle of Quiet* (San Francisco: Harper & Row, 1972) 28.

Chapter One

[1] Robert Short, *The Gospel According to Peanuts* (Richmond, VA: John Knox Press, 1964) 114.
[2] Cited in Roger L. Shinn, *Man: The New Humanism* (Philadelphia: Westminster Press, 1967) 69–70.

Chapter Two

[1] *The Immense Journey* (New York: Vintage Books, 1946) 122–23.

Chapter Three

[1] Robert Short, *The Parables of Peanuts* (New York: Harper & Row, 1968) 287–88.
[2] *The Rubaiyat of Omar Khayyam.*
[3] *Miracles* (New York: Macmillan Publishing Company, 1978).
[4] Cited in James S. Stewart, *The Strong Name* (New York: Charles Scribner's Sons, 1941) 147.
[5] Ibid., 154.

Chapter Four

[1] "Modern Civilization's Crucial Problem," in *Riverside Sermons* (New York: Harper & Brothers, 1958) 241.
[2] Rita Snowden, in William Barclay, *And He Had Compassion on Them* (Edinburgh: The Church of Scotland Youth Committee) 169.

Chapter Five

[1] Cited in Martin E. Marty, *A Cry of Absence* (San Francisco: Harper & Row, 1983) 17–18.
[2] Frederick B. Speakman, *The Salty Tang* (Westwood, New Jersey: Fleming H. Revell Company, 1954) 97.
[3] *Key Next Door* (London: Hodder and Stoughton, 1959) 122.

Chapter Six

[1] Cited in John Killinger, *The Thickness of Glory* (New York: Abingdon, 1964) 91–92.
[2] "The Nature and Ground of Christian Hope Today," *Christianity & Crisis*, 6 June 1988, 204.
[3] *God Is No Fool* (Nashville: Abingdon Press, 1969).
[4] (New York: Viking Press, 1964).
[5] Cited in Morton Kelsey, *Afterlife* (New York: Paulist Press, 1979) 179.

Chapter Seven

[1] *The Healing of Persons* (New York: Harper & Row, 1965) 225.
[2] *Surprised by Joy* (New York: Harcourt, Brace and World, 1955) 226.
[3] *Key Next Door*, 194.
[4] "The Rime of the Ancient Mariner," in I. A. Richards, ed., *The Portable Coleridge* (New York: Penguin Books, 1977) 98.

Chapter Eight

[1] (New York: Perennial Library, Harper & Row, 1985) 220–21.
[2] "Needing the Unexpectable," in Rushworth Kidder, ed., *An Agenda for the 21st Century* (Cambridge, MA: The MIT Press, 1988) 149–156.
[3] *The Greening of the Church* (Waco, TX: Work Books, 1971) 69–70.

Chapter Nine

[1] (Garden City, NY: Nelson Doubleday, Inc.) 10.

Chapter Ten

[1] *I Believe* (Philadelphia: Fortress Press, 1968) 136.
[2] "To a Waterfowl," in Nancy Sullivan, ed., *The Treasury of American Poetry* (Garden City, NY: Doubleday & Company, Inc., 1978) 58.
[3] *Signposts for the Future* (Garden City, NY: Doubleday and Company, 1978) 108.
[4] Alfred Barbou, *Victor Hugo and His Time,* trans. Ellen E. Frewer (New York: Harper & Brothers, 1882) 254.
[5] *Death: The Final Stage of Growth* (Englewood Cliffs, NJ: Prentice-Hall, Inc., 1975) 19.